DATE DUE

NOV 2 6 1994				
OCT 0 1 2001				
SEP 1 5 2005				

TEMPLE

BOOKS BY GEORGE DENNISON

Luisa Domic and Shawno

Temple

A Tale of Pierrot and Other Stories

Oilers and Sweepers and Other Stories

The Lives of Children

And Then a Harvest Feast

TEMPLE

GEORGE DENNISON

EDITED BY GEOFFREY GARDNER
AND TAYLOR STOEHR

STEERFORTH PRESS
SOUTH ROYALTON, VERMONT

For information about permission to reproduce selections
from this book, write to: Steerforth Press L.C., P.O. Box 70,
South Royalton, Vermont 05068.

Library of Congress Cataloging-in-Publication Data
Dennison, George 1925–
Temple / George Dennison ; edited by Geoffrey Gardner and Taylor Stoehr.
p.   cm.
ISBN 1–883642–22–1
1. Dennison, George, 1925–   —Homes and haunts—Maine—Temple.
2. Authors, American—20th century—Biography.
3. Temple (Me.)—Social life and customs
I. Gardner, Geoffrey, 1943– . II. Stoehr, Taylor, 1931– . III. Title.
PS3554.E55Z47   1994
818′.5403—dc20   94–10060

Excerpts from "Essay" from *Collected Shorter Poems 1946–1991*.
Copyright © 1992 by Hayden Carruth. Used by permission of
Copper Canyon Press, P.O. Box 271, Port Townsend, WA 98368.

Manufactured in the United States of America

First Edition

[PREFACE]

When George Dennison moved to the little town of Temple in the heart of rural Maine, it was the last of a series of events that marked a major turning-point in his life. For almost twenty years he had lived as a bohemian—what he called a "wastrel" life—chiefly in Manhattan but with stretches in Mexico, Hollywood, and Hoboken, New Jersey, trying to make himself a writer. He had sold one story, but it had never been published. Although his plays had been produced by groups of friends in lofts, and by the Judson Poets Theater in Greenwich Village, the audience for them was minuscule. A few essays and reviews had appeared in literary journals, and some gallery criticism in *Art News,* but it was not much to show for so many years of effort. Meanwhile he had supported himself as a day laborer, a house painter, a prep school teacher, a therapist for disturbed children, a hack writer of TV scripts. Two marriages had ended badly.

In the mid-sixties Dennison's friend Paul Goodman had introduced him to Mabel Chrystie, a young woman with a passion for children and free schools, who was starting a storefront school—The First Street School—on the lower east side of Manhattan. Dennison joined the staff as a part-time teacher and therapist for the older boys. The journal he kept during the next two years ultimately became *The Lives of Children,* still widely regarded as the best book to come out of the free school movement. By the time the book was published in 1969 the school was closed for lack of funds, but Dennison and Mabel

Chrystie had married and had their first child. Soon they decided to leave the increasingly desperate wastes of New York to raise their family in Maine.

Coming to Temple meant leaving the world of high culture and bohemian life, the scene of so many years of poverty and frustration as an artist, of passion and despair as a lover. There was much in all this Dennison never could quite say good-bye to—periodically it drew him back—but he was in many ways a new man. He was well known now as a writer, no longer balked by self-doubt. He was a husband with a wife and child—and with two more to come—transported to a difficult but absolutely gorgeous world of forest, farms, streams, and sky.

The Dennisons lived a few miles from town, up a long road that climbed steeply through dense woods and then broke out into an upland meadow where an old farmhouse and barns stood overlooking the valley, Mount Blue in the far distance. At first they did without electricity and most modern conveniences, keeping warm with several small woodstoves and lighting with kerosene lamps. Slowly they built the place up, hiring local craftsmen and doing much of the labor themselves. They started a parent-run free school. They entered into both the counter-cultural flux of other urban expatriates and also the small town web of neighborliness: barter, mutual aid, and conversation.

Dennison had his own little cabin ten minutes' walk further up the hill, to which he would retreat for days at a time, to write and paint, or simply to escape the community life which grew up thick around his wife. At times he hated the isolation and boredom of the country, at other times he hated the throng in his house—not the local people, but visitors from the city or the new settlers like himself, who came up the road to borrow tools or vehicles, or to take a bath, eat a meal, and often spend the night. He loved Temple and his life there, but he raged against it too and sometimes jumped in the car and drove off to Boston or New York in a panic of revulsion from the cultural backwater of the woods and longing for the bright lights and sophisticated talk of the city. One could see that although there had been changes since his wastrel days, his economy of spirit remained much the same.

It took many years to make peace with himself, but he gradually steadied and finally, like the rest of his family, he too began to put down roots. The transformation drew on a number of sources, perhaps the most important was his love for his children, which blossomed in him and filled him with joy. It was crucial too that his writing had been going better ever since *The Lives of Children*. He still wrote in flurries and binges, but he could bring things to completion now, and with each new work discovered further powers and confidence. Age also made a difference. And finally among the factors must be counted Temple itself, the healing beauty of woods and streams, and the heroic virtues of its natives.

It was out of these benignant influences that the present book comes.

In the beginning it was a lark. Early in the autumn of 1976 Dennison, who had been working on a good many paintings up in his cabin studio, found himself entranced by the changing colors of the leaves, and he made himself a new notebook in which he would daily write down the palette he saw spreading through the trees. Soon this expanded to an account of other turns in the season, and it became a portrait of country life, both lyric and gritty, a Bruegel. In the spring he did it again; and thereafter for a few years, though steadily diminishing in scale, he set down in six little handmade notebooks his journal of the seasons.

Meanwhile the rural life he led was more and more taking over his fiction. He wrote a novella, *Shawno*, about a dog he had owned in New York, but the scene was Maine and he put his family and their neighbors in it. He borrowed passages from his journal of the seasons for another, less fictionalized sketch of life in Temple, "Family Pages: Little Facts," and then, when he was writing his chief work of this period, *Luisa Domic*, he lifted much of the same material out of this piece and the journals to fill out the idyllic world into which the political horrors of the coup in Chile come crashing.

It was not just the cycle of the seasons that furnished these new works. Dennison had also begun, a few years after the first journals, to seek out his neighbors and record their lives and characters in much the same way he reported on the landscape they lived in. He called these "interviews," as indeed they sometimes were, though more often they were conversations taking place over some ordinary mutual activity—splitting logs, slaughtering sheep, playing poker, buying an axe handle, or gentling a startled horse. Unlike the seasonal journals, these interviews were written down on separate sheets of paper—rarely more than one or two pages, but in Dennison's tiniest handwriting so they often contained quite lengthy accounts—and with a number of his neighbors there were repeated visits and writings. When he had filled his page, he merely stuffed it in a drawer with the rest, in no particular order.

As these accumulated along with his seasons, and as he found ways of working them into his fiction, it dawned on him that they were in themselves a project he had undertaken, and that they might form the basis for a still bigger and more ambitious book than *Luisa Domic*. He began to think of this new project as "Fontayne" (named for one of the local men he admired, Eddie Fontayne), or simply as "The Maine Book." It was to be a comic epic with many story lines, full of farcical episodes and tall tales, but underlying the humor would be this plain ground of sober browns and black, the hard, heroic, tragic life going forward all around him.

The conception matured in him very slowly, over six or eight years. Although he scribbled "Fontayne" in the corner of more and more notes to himself, often just scraps—little jokes, bits of dialogue, impressions and facts of life in the fields and woods—he never wrote down anything like a plan or outline. Nonetheless much of it had already taken shape in his imagination by the end of 1986. He had his main characters in mind, their situations and relations to one another. He had not invented a single narrative thread to hold the book together, for it was to be a picaresque. And he had not yet confronted the problem of how the comic scenes would sit against the backdrop of the seasons and the drama of youth and age, struggle, suffering and death, which— again as in a Bruegel painting—lay just under the surface of all his interviews and journals. That would come, if it could, in the writing.

And then in the early weeks of 1987 Dennison discovered he had cancer. The rest of his life—he died the following October—was devoted to taking leave of the world he loved: family, friends, art, nature. When we came that summer to help him pack up and label his papers, which characteristically lay on the tables and chairs and floor of his room, strewn and heaped like the leaves of autumn, we found many little yellow notes, two by three inches, marked "Fontayne." There were also four drawers, high in the bank of drawers against one wall, in which all the interviews were laid away. He could see them from his bed, with windows and sky behind them. "Don't box those," he said to us. "That would be too much like a burial."

It was a long time after he died before we took those pages out of the drawers and looked at them. We found there was no connected narrative in them at all, no more than a few pages at a time that seemed to carry on continuously. But as we examined the interviews more closely and held them up against the seasonal journals, which Dennison had kept in other drawers, we saw a new possibility. It would certainly not be the comic epic he had planned, but perhaps there was a book there after all, a kind of picture gallery of life in rural Maine.

So we transcribed the interviews and tried to find an order for them that would unfold without confusing a reader, and we inter- leaved his seasons in a rhythm that seemed right to us. We have only very rarely and lightly touched the prose itself, which was already in Dennison's best and fullest voice.

In *Temple* the seasons go their round—ice-fishing on the ponds in winter, spring floods sinking the road under three feet of water, the annual slaughtering of sheep, autumn brush cutting at the cemetery. Dennison pulls us back in time too, retracing the horse-and-buggy milk run with ninety-year-old Dana Hamlin, who drove his team year after year in all weathers. Dennison lets us listen in on the reminiscences of the town selectmen, bantering through their weekly poker game together. We meet Eddie Fontayne himself, the French-Canadian woodworker who carves fiddles as well as axe handles and fumes at his failing eyesight, his bad leg, and the steady advance of his own mortality. And Mr. Fife, a backroads eccentric who surely knows the best way to do each task, from pruning trees to frying leeks. We visit with Esther who has spent her life and modest resources caring for fellow creatures—dogs bred for sale, goats for milk, horses for saddle and work, her neighbors' ailing cattle, elderly wards of the state, and her own children and foster children.

Dennison's interest in these encounters is not nostalgic. Under his hand these local lives take on the dimensions of myth or legend. In *Luisa Domic*, Dennison's narrator—to a great extent an avatar of Dennison himself—says the following about a project which is very much like the pages we are offering here:

> I had a shoebox of loose papers I had been carrying from the house to the cabin and back to the house again. It was filled with notes of conversations with my neighbors. I had made them over a period of years, not with any purpose but in a reflex of savoring; and then I had come to see that they comprised a subject. What I had taken to be nostalgia wasn't that at all. My neighbors' vanished life—the small farms, the crosscut saws and axes, the teams of horses and oxen, the ten-cow herds, the modest orchards, the sheep, hens, and kitchen gardens, the water-powered mills—that life had *used* them powerfully and had rewarded them, not by any means abundantly, but nevertheless along a spectrum of human motives. . . . They spoke of it in praise.

Finally and most insistently, we come back again and again to the recurrent motif that underscores the precariousness of all this natural and human abundance—the men who work in the woods, the most dangerous of local callings, their scarred faces, missing limbs, blinded eyes, and their helpless anger at the lumber companies and paper mills that set prices high and wages low while rising insurance and tax rates eat up the livelihood of families.

"I love these old ones," Dennison once wrote, "who knew a way of life and have virtues and are dying." Twenty years of reconnoitering in the dooryards, workshops, and woodlots of his neighbors come to fruition in this prolonged meditation on the traditional community that was vanishing before his eyes. It is at once a celebration and a lament for the self-reliant culture of America that now exists less and less anywhere but in the imagination.

GEOFFREY GARDNER
TAYLOR STOEHR

[JOURNAL]

OCTOBER 4

These days are so beautiful it's almost painful. Many leaves still green—beech and sugar maple and brown ash—though even these, in certain locations, have begun to pale and blush. The red maples (swamp maples) have turned their deep magenta, hot magenta, heart's blood magenta. The white birch and poplar leaves have turned golden ochre, deliciously pale and glowing, especially looking up and seeing them against the pale blue sky at evening (the sun sets abruptly, the temperature drops abruptly—from warm to quite cool; frost at night).

The road to the cabin dazzlingly beautiful at all hours of the day, the tall trees (maples and ash, shorter beeches) almost meeting at the top, and so thick and leafy that the blue of the sky appears in flecks and fragments, intense and dazzling scattered everywhere among those sunlit ochres, magentas, rusty orange and golden green.

The insects are gone (a few feeble mosquitoes and, of course, the Lazarus flies, their dreadful buzzing and torn wings), and many birds have gone, though one frequently hears birds. The sun is strong but without edge, persistent, enveloping, not piercing, a *baking* sun; everything is still. The dogs loll on the grass, or sit long whiles blinking slowly. I look at the hills, putter in the garden, look at the hills, split wood, look at the hills. Finally I get into the car and drive to Wilder Hill, walking the last mile. Only a fragment of the former sweeping view—all grown up in scrub—a more beautiful vista right at the house—but the beautiful day is everywhere, one can't go wrong. I drive to Drury Pond and for an hour paddle slowly in the leaking canoe, watching the hills slowly rear up behind me (and thinking of Wordsworth's description of this in *The Prelude*). The pond is surrounded by hills, incredible to look at. The water is high, at least a foot and a half higher than ever before—because of the beaver dam at the outlet. They have a spillway at one of the inlets, too, and are very busy in the swamp beyond it.

Mabel and the kids and I ate a picnic supper at the pond the previous night—I took Becky, Michael, and Susie out in the canoe. It was dusk. We were at the far side of the pond and looked back and saw the rippling sharp wedge, lengthening and widening, of a swimming beaver. It heard our excited voices, *thwapped* the water with its tail and plunged under.

Partridge near the cabin, flushed by the dogs. A crisp, cold October night, with stars and a frost.

I saw many filaments of the spiders today, the long strands they throw out for migrating. Some lay across the grass. I was stretched out near the cabin and saw a strand attached at one end to a low weed, maybe eighteen inches high, the other end—four or five feet—lifting and falling gently, sensitive to the merest whisper of air. The sun caught it from time to time, always a new shape, changing constantly. And then in the canoe, in the inlet of the pond, I caught the long, sinuous drifting glint of such a strand a few feet above my head, the spider clung to one end and was airborne. I had never seen such a thing before, though I had read of the magnetism of spiders and of the black spiders sighted by pilots at great heights.

I have the seat and back of a kitchen chair on the front seat of the Saab—first comfortable arrangement.

OCTOBER 5

Mr. Kidd came with the wood, a cord cut and split, up to the cabin. He had a shotgun in the front seat. "I haven't seen any birds."

I: "You will . . . maybe. Split with me?" I showed him where the partridge had been. He stalked through the trees a while, but without luck.

The field corn quite dry on the stalk. Mabel forgot it was still there and let the ponies in to eat the witch grass. So I went down to gather it. The ponies were just discovering it. I yelled and chased them. They had forgotten where they came in, couldn't find the exit—typical pony panic. I picked the corn—cut my thumb badly on the sharp dry husks—tossing it into the garden cart, kicking over each stalk so I'd know where I'd been. The pumpkins were curing at their end of the cornfield. There were a few acorn squash we'd missed, visible now among the dead leaves.

Another beautiful day. Mabel had farmed out Michael and was working in the garden. We debated what to do where all the witch grass had come in. She wanted to rototill it. I thought there was no point in that, it would all come up in the spring, multiplied. "More efficient—in the long run—to dig it up with the fork and shake out the soil." (We throw the witch grass—its incredible roots—on the dirt road, where it gets mashed and withers.)

I husked the field corn out of the cart by the uphill porch. The ponies stood near. I fed them tips, silk, unripened ears. Both are fat and velvety. I tied the good ears in pairs and stacked them on a burlap bag. The ponies kept sidling closer to that stack. The dogs were lolling near. Every time I yelled at the ponies the dogs leaped up and flew at them, anxious for a chance to chase them. I had to call the dogs off, particularly Sashka, who loves to run the ponies and will drive them far into the woods. Shem got on Starbright's heels and miscalculated and Starbright wheeled unexpectedly and kicked him in the shoulder.

The hollow, resonant crunching of the ponies beside me as I worked. Looking often at the orange and green hills.

Kirsten, the teacher's daughter, at supper. I came in from the cabin (where I'd snatched an hour and a half of work) and I mentioned the partridge.

Becky: "If you shoot a partridge I'll kill you, daddy."

Susie: "Don't shoot any partridge. They didn't do anything to you."

Kirsten: "Let them live as long as they would."

I: "But you eat hamburger."

Susie: "Only a little bit and not often."

I: "And what about you, Becky? You ate Willy-Woo last winter. You said, Willy-Woo is dead and I'm glad. Just because he butted you. Would it be okay to kill a partridge if he weighed 500 pounds and tried to butt me? Did you ever hear a 500-pound canary?"

Becky (like a huge frog): "CHIRP!"

I helped with the dishes. Mabel kept smiling, kept trying to pick a fight—that is, playing at it verbally, a kind of banter.

Mabel: "It's surprising how people cling to their kitchen habits."

I: "Like what? What have I done?"

Mabel: "I hate the way you soak dishes. And there's a folded paper bag in the pantry."

I: "Oh my God! There *is?*"

She giggles. She inadvertently kicks over three bottles from a phalanx of twelve on the floor.

I: "You only got three. I'll set them up."

She giggles.

The night sky quite light, the moon (almost full—gibbous) behind an even veil of scruffy, mottled clouds. No stars at all. The clouds cover the entire sky.

OCTOBER 6

Rain, mist. The clouds, or mist, hang down over the hills, obscuring the tops, so that on all sides there seems to be a forested swell, an undulating plain of orange and green. Dripping rain at daybreak, overcast now, wet, but no drops.

Intermittent light showers all day.

I drive to Waterville to take pants to tailor to be let out, shoes to shoemaker. I pass three men digging a culvert ditch across the road. One is in the ditch. Two standing, one of whom has an enormous Falstaffian belly, clad all in gray, with brown rubber boots and black and red hunting cap.

I dislike Waterville, but it's better than Rumford. It's unpleasant to leave the hills and woods and go out into the small cities and towns.

I took Becky and Susie to the high school (a far more sumptuous establishment than we could ever have imagined when I was young) to see *The World of Gilbert and Sullivan*—five Britishers touring in the States, singing excerpts from the operas. They weren't bad, but not splendid either. The peculiar forlorn feeling of such occasions: everyone understands that the real thing is unattainable, too costly, we don't have the style for it; and everyone sees that the essential audience-actor relationship isn't there: these are strangers. We get bits and pieces.

We left at intermission. I rushed to Dick Blodgett's house to watch the last hour of the Ford-Carter debate. One doesn't expect information, or truth, or reasoned argument—only some sense of what the man is like. Ford is not smart, is insecure, a dummy, actually, guarding every word but blundering. Carter smarter, more human, one believes he does have moral feelings—but his real policies are obscure. And I wonder: will the Americans choose Ford because he *is* a sort of a metal-and-plastic Caliban, a small-scale monster? Do they *want* a monster and monstrous politics precisely because they don't want to be involved? Perhaps no one believes anymore in such entities as "the nation," "national life," "national purpose." They were (are) horrid lies.

To go from close contact with the dogs, ponies, trees, etc. to the words and movement, the faces and clothing of the TV is to suffer a terrible loss of soul; life is diminished instantaneously.

Driving over the wet roads at night, many leaves down in the rain, black dully-glistening tar surface, mist ahead and on both sides. I see again and again a tiny frog leaping across the road . . . LEAP-plop . . . LEAP-plop . . . LEAP-plop . . . going high into the air and dropping foolishly just to get ahead ten or twelve inches, incredibly inefficient and in this setting (not lily pads) forlorn.

OCTOBER 7

The mist has lifted, though the sky is partly overcast and dull. But the lifting of the mist reveals the hills, and they are much lighter, more yellow-and-orange than before. As often, a serious change of weather at full moon (or near) accompanied by—to some degree—storm. More leaves down on the road to my cabin.

Stalwart, spooky, Greg Butler going off into the woods with a hunting bow in one hand, a quiver of arrows strapped to the exact middle of his back.

Ted tells me Johnny Grant is in the hospital again. He has been given up for dead so many times in the last ten years no one knows what to think. He was in intensive care, but is better now and receiving visitors.

I spent the morning making bread and puttering in the house. Late afternoon I took my pistol and went up to the cabin, hoping to flush some partridge on the way—not that I could very likely hit one in flight . . . maybe on the ground.

The colors of October! The ferns by the road are still green, or rather chartreuse, the grass a bronze green—and the new grass in the field Thorndike sowed for us is a yellow green. The milkweed in the fields and the fluff of the ragweed are brownish gray, and dull. The colors of the leaves are saturated colors, and there is so much light coming through the leaves (like stained glass windows) that they glow—hence the ubiquitous adjectives: flaming, blazing, burning.

The young trees, the saplings and seedlings, retain green in their leaves longer than the mature trees. The largest leaves in the woods were those of little moosewood seedlings no more than two feet high. The leaves were pale green, translucent, eight to ten inches across.

The reds of the maples:

blood	apples
salmon	pomegranates
cranberry	roses

Part of the mysterious effect of these colored leaves is that one doesn't quite know where the colored *surface* is. There are many, many surfaces, and all are suffused with light—the result is a haze, a dense mist of color.

Some of the maple ochres have an *absorbent* look, soaking up color, soaking up light. The advanced stage of the magenta of the swamp maples is like tobacco—red leather—the leaves fall then, and these dark, rich splotches appear against the rusty saffrons and golds of poplars and birch. Beside the road are little seedlings, eight to twenty inches high, and their green ochre leaves seem bright against the mixed colors of the fallen leaves.

Of the maples, birches, poplar, ash—which go in spectra of yellow, tan, with sometimes intermixures of red: amber, saffron, ochre, golden-green, buckskin, sand, mahogany. There were ash leaves on the path as dark as tobacco, or richly darkened leather.

Given the saturation of these colors, and their strange insubstantiality, that is both hot and cool, their breathtaking effect on the hills is due to their remarkable combinations, which include great contrasts as well as subtle gradations and continuities. The burning deep-orange-tan will appear beside the blood red magenta and both will be set off against the dark blue-greens and dark shadows of spruce, fir, and pine. The brilliant ochres appear everywhere and seem to mediate between the reds at one end and the greens at the other. Other combinations: golden green against ochre; magenta against golden green; young ash leaves almost black, their ox-blood red is so deep, against the golden green of young maples. Some of the ash trees are bare already. The huge old sugar maples in the thick of the woods (once they were the roadside trees of the old farm road that went on past the orchards, now dead) are massive great towers of flaming reds, ochres, salmon, rust.

At the turn to my cabin, opposite the collapsing old farmhouse, grape vines have run wild and now there are clusters of purple and mauve grapes dangling from the topmost limbs of the apple tree, now almost dead, which ten years ago, when I first came here, bore excellent McIntosh apples. How will I get the grapes down? I probably won't. There is so much here that one simply can't cope with. Waste, rot and death everywhere, and an abiding sense of one's own mortality, far more, all of this, than one ever dreams of, living in a city. It's bearable because fertility outweighs it and also seems endless.

The day was warm and still. Any plans one might have had had already been picked apart by the super-laziness of this time between seasons, time out of time. I stalked through the old orchard in the woods, imagining that I was hunting partridge—so dazzled and strangely at peace (torporous yet restless; restless, yet without desire or discontent) that it was like walking through the landscape of a fantasy or dream, or re-enacting something that had happened many, many years ago. I could as well have leaned against a tree and slept as have gone on walking.

I saw a red squirrel thirty yards away on the stone wall, upright, holding perfectly still. Over the years I've shot maybe a dozen to keep them away from the house, because of rabies and their destructiveness. And so I shot this one—through the head at the first shot—not really fearing his rabies or worried about his destructiveness. And, as creatures, I like them. He was cold dead, not even twitching, by the time I got to him. Sour, acidic depression, guilt, anxiety, sorrow—mild forms of all of these—the appalling difference between life and death. And how upset the children would be at this! I didn't really know why I had done it—simply having the gun in my hand, and the motive already set, my hunt for partridge. I thought of the relative innocence of relation to the woods and animals of the vegetarians I know, and remembered killing a bird when I was a child, stalking with a bow and arrow; and my own children's discovery of death and their protective affection for small creatures. And that very night I read a poem of Hayden's beginning "So many poems about the deaths of animals" and saying,

> . . . *This*
> *has been the time of the finishing off of the animals.*
> *. . . I have lived with them fifty years,*
> *we have lived with them fifty million years,*
> *and now they are going, almost gone. I don't know*
> *if the animals are capable of reproach.*
> *But clearly they do not bother to say good-bye.*

This little death stays with me. There is something appalling in it. One moment the creature is continuous with everything and possesses, in its own terms, a world, and the next moment it is nothing, rather mere matter, localized and inert.

Lettuce, collards, kale, cabbage, a few other things still doing well in the garden. All the tomatoes were brought in ten days ago and are ripening on the work counter by the window. It was a small crop— nothing in boxes in the root cellar.

A fresh salad for supper. Lorna Wilkinson is coming next week on her way back to England. The house has never been messier—the accumulation of Michael's first two years. I've agreed to babysit after supper so that Mabel can either sleep or work alone. And the kids and I will clean up after supper. Becky was at Jesse's. It was warm outside, and still. The ponies stood in the darkness right at the door, pressing their noses against the screen. After we had eaten I went outside with Susie and Michael and fed the dogs. Susie and I sat on the wooden table in the yard, just a few feet from the dogs, and watched them eat. The ponies stood near, watching them too. It had been unpleasant in the house, I'd felt irritable there—couldn't tell if because of Mabel, or atmospheric pressure or full moon, or just something in me—but outdoors it was pleasant. I held Michael in my lap, and he was peaceful.

After the dogs ate they wrestled together a long long while right at our feet. Starbright, looking huge with his pre-winter fat, brushed right by the dogs to eat the leftovers in Sashka's bowl. Susie picked it up and put it under the table. Starbright came close, nudging my arm and shoulder, just as Shem does, wanting to be petted. But he has never done this with me before. We stayed there a long while watching the dogs, talking, petting the pony, Michael slowly drowsing off to sleep. I carried him inside and we put a blanket over him on the sofa, and Susie and I sat beside him and looked at her math book. Then she read to me a couple of pages from *The Fellowship of the Ring,* and I took it up and read several pages to her, and she fell asleep. It was about 9:15. I washed dishes and scoured pots until 11:20, and then walked in the moonlight up to the cabin.

The moon was so bright that from my cabin door I could see the orange leaves of the sugar maples seventy yards away by the old house. Lots of animal sounds, dogs barking in the distance, owls in the woods, and a brief squawking that I couldn't identify, a large bird of some kind.

OCTOBER 8

Rain again. Chuck was going to come today to help me move firewood indoors. There are great stacks of it in front of the house. But I don't want to take it in while it's wet. I ate breakfast here at the cabin and sat in the doorway with my coffee and watched the rain. The handsome large pine right there at the door was shedding raindrops and old needles at the same time. The old needles are straw-colored. They grow—and fall—in clusters of five, all held at one end, the way a Japanese fan is. Many of the falling needles catch on other needles and small branches of the tree, and will hang there until the first strong wind. From a short distance these hanging needles, and the clusters of dead needles yet to fall, form a faint, straw-colored haze or veil over the deep green of the tree.

I stack part of the cord of split stove wood under the overhanging cabin roof. Pleasant to be here and to work lazily at these notes, stopping occasionally to stack wood, or to read some poems of Hayden's, several of which are extremely good. One batch (he xeroxed the galleys) would have been a New Directions book (they've done four or five books of his), but they cancelled it at the last minute. He sent out sets to fifteen friends. I doubt if any American poetry of the last year is better. The other batch was in *American Poetry Review*. Michael Rothchild made xeroxes for me. Here too were poems as good as anyone is writing in this country. And Hayden is hard put to make ends meet!

I had told Mabel I would come down after supper (wasn't hungry) and read to the kids. Evening coming on—dusk—as I walked down. The all-day rain has added a great many leaves to the road, there is orange, red, yellow everywhere, above, to both sides, in front, and underfoot. The white trunks of birches glow against the foliage in this dim light; and the wet trunks of ash and cherry look black.

Susie told me that Mabel, Becky, and Michael were at the Kimbers cutting and weighing cheese for the co-op.

She said, "I saw some geese this morning, but they weren't flying in a V, they were in a line, and they were going up and down like, you know those bobbers on the ocean . . ."

Me: "Buoys?"

Susie: "Yeah, buoys . . . it was like they were all on a string and going up and down on the water."

This was a marvelously accurate and pretty way to say it. She had asked me just the night before what a poem was—they were doing poems at school. I told her that this description was very close to being a poem. Later I got a pencil and paper, she began to sing it, and with scarcely any revision we arrived at:

> *Geese,*
> *when they are flying south*
> *are like a string*
> *of bobbins/going up and down/*
> *on the deep*
> *wide ocean.*

Becky, all this while, was leaning against me and trying to interrupt. I made a clean copy of the poem and gave it to Susie, and Becky ran and brought me more paper and said she wanted to write one too. So I got ready for dictation. She giggled, looked this way and that, and kept saying, "Uh . . . uh . . . uh . . ." I said, "It was easy for Susie because she told me about something she saw, and she sang it. Did you see anything special today?"

Becky: "I don't know . . . "

I: "Sing me a song about the rain, or all the colors of the leaves . . . "

She said, "Okay," and immediately sang:

> *When the days are orange*
> *the leaves*
> *are falling down.*

Mabel and I both said how nice it was, and so she went on and sang several others:

> *I like to play*
> *the bells*
> *when they go*
> *ding, ding, ding.*

And,

> *I like the winter*
> *I hate the winter*
> *I like the winter because*
> *I get to slide*
> *down the nice steep hills,*
> *I hate the winter*
> *because it's so frozen cold.*

And a couple of others ("I like it when Susie and mom make nice warm fires.") all composed sitting on the arm of the big chair I was in, and bouncing and wiggling so much, always leaning against me, I had to say again and again, don't bounce my arm, I can't write. This time it was Susie's turn to try to interrupt.

I read to Becky from *Little Town on the Prairie,* the chapter called
"Fourth of July," in which an orator says with great spirit how we
licked the British despot, and then reads the Declaration of
Independence—such rousing language, such whopping anger and
pride, I had to stop. I was crying. I cried before, two years ago, reading
the same passage to Susie. How we all suffer from being disgusted with
our so-called leaders, ashamed of our country, alienated from one
another! The time of nations is over. But it *was* a great day when men
freed themselves of kings and princes, and could own their farms. And
our leaders were able to speak then, and could write a sentence with
both feeling and thought in it. Compared to this, our paranoiac public
style, presidents unable to talk *freely,* much less with feeling, everyone
mouthing clichés, hiding all the time. Agh!

OCTOBER 9

Heavy rain, very heavy, began around 5:00 in the morning. Mabel had
to leave at 7:30 to take Michael to the dentist. She'd been worrying
about it, the difficulty of holding him for the drilling of cavities—the
possibility of hospital. The rain was so heavy I was afraid the road
might flood, especially since the beavers have thrown up a larger-than-
ever dam across the outlet from the pond, and the pond itself was
reaching road level at two places. The rain kept coming down harder. I
got up at 6:00 and drove down to check the lower road. It was O.K.

Becky, Susie, and I had breakfast together. Becky is feisty, cheerful,
but quarrelsome at breakfast. Susie fries an egg for her and says, "Get
me a bowl while you're getting yours."

"Get it yourself," says tough Becky. Mabel and Michael came back
from the dentist as we were finishing, happy, as no drilling had been
needed after all.

There is still green in some of the poplar leaves, but even the
birches now are quite yellow and orange. Elm leaves are down, and
many ash leaves. The wild cherries are a deep yellow-green. There is
still quite a lot of green on the locusts, though about half of the leaves

GEORGE DENNISON

are fading to ochre, especially on the smaller trees. The locusts come into leaf later than most other trees, too.

In the afternoon I drove Becky and Michael through heavy rain to Zoe's birthday party at David's little cabin/house in Avon. Zoe, Pita, Aziza, a little girl I didn't know (and her mother), and Kim, David's new girlfriend.

Later at the party Jack Carson and Joe Dankowski came, and Charlie Adams and an Old Crow Band pot-head friend simmering with spite and rancor under the patina of intoxication. I can't stand being around these people very long. I left soon with Michael. Becky stayed to spend the night with Zoe.

So many marriages are on the rocks here. Dick and Craigon (Dick is living at Charlie's); Jack and Christine; Norman and Sue; Chuck and Jeannie . . . others. The co-counselling has hastened it.

Michael fell asleep in the car going home. He loves music. He had begun calling for Mabel, but as soon as I began singing, he simply sat there and listened, sometimes joined, and eventually dozed off.

OCTOBER 11

A beautiful day, but cold, a little windy. Now some of the white maples are bare, and there are many more bare branches everywhere, but the sugar maples are blazing in the sunlight, so bright one almost doubts one's eyes. The cabin road is entirely carpeted with orange leaves.

Chuck has come with his truck to move some wood into the cellar. Tall, slow, puzzled, suffering from the difficulties of life here (boredom and the terrible scarcity of jobs) and suffering especially from the failure of his marriage. He works slowly, but steadily . . . and is so unhappy he can't keep instructions straight in his head and wastes two hours in an error I specifically cautioned him against.

Late afternoon, the windows in the big room show amazing bands of color: orange (the maples halfway up the distant hills), dark green, blue green (the spruce and fir at the top of the hills), deep blue sky, pearly clouds, deep blue again, pearly white.

14

I worked all day shoveling manure and pulling it hither and yon in the cart. Tired at night. Becky was irritating. I read *Fellowship of the Ring* to Susie and went to bed early, just after she fell asleep with her head on my shoulder. Neither she nor Becky will admit she's falling asleep, so we have a rule: If I think they are too drowsy to understand, I quiz them on the last paragraph; if they fail the quiz, it's time for bed.

OCTOBER 12

A severe freeze last night, temperatures down to 20, but the sky is light today. As usual, the beginning of cold weather finds us unprepared: car radiators, cellar-vent holes, etc.

At breakfast: Michael rigged out in thrift-shop fandango, clothes Mabel would never consider buying at a store: polka dot overalls, bright tweed jacket (but still barefoot). We were all laughing at it, Michael enjoying the laughter. Susie said, "He's a pretty fancy baby!" Mabel: "He's not a baby anymore, he's a kid." And Michael said, "Me kid." I held out my arms to him and said, "Come, Michael, uppie."

Michael: "No uppie."

Me: "Daddy uppie Michael."

He ran away laughing and saying, "No uppie," as I chased him. Then I said, "Michael uppie daddy," and he chortled with delight at the thought of it, and said in a different tone, shaking his head, "No uppie."

There's a new woodchuck hole in back of the house. Sashka dug frantically at it—the creature was inside—but those tunnels really work. A hazard to the ponies, who still make those marvelous end-of-the-day sprints around and around the house, down the field and up the road.

The road to the cabin is deep in leaves now, and two days of wind have made them dry and crinkly. The wind blew a good size poplar down across the road, just uphill of the generator.

OCTOBER 13

I slept at the cabin last night and woke up to the sound of partridge drumming, not far off in the woods.

A cool day, thick fog. We're expecting Lorna Wilkinson on her way back to England, but if the fog doesn't lift the flights will be cancelled at Augusta.

The fog did lift. I took the kids with me and drove to Augusta for Lorna. She must be in her middle sixties—lively, attractive, intelligent-looking, wearing an elegant fur coat, yet looking equal to anything that might come up. She spent two years in a Japanese prison camp in the Philippines.

And she wasn't coming from Canada at all, but straight from London, an impromptu vacation to make up for a cancelled cruise with friends. She has good friends a few hours from here, on the coast, and will spend a week with them before going back.

Rain at night.

More wood from Mr. Kidd.

OCTOBER 14

Windy, sunny, with hurled handfuls of sparkling drops of rain. Huge white clouds and deep blue sky (the same sky that I saw in Scotland, which Ivan says was—with Maine—all the same land mass eons ago).

The wind will dry the wood. I've been stacking it here at the cabin. When the piles are dry down at the house, we'll move more into the cellar.

From noon on, high wind, leaves sailing from west to east. Dark storm clouds at the horizon; straight above the clouds are white and the sky blue.

Late afternoon we walked with Lorna through the woods to Porter Hill to meet Susie and Becky on their way home from school, and to show Lorna the school. Storm threatening, but the damp high wind was invigorating.

We gathered grapes from the raggedy vines on the old Porter Hill farm. They were getting leathery, but were still worth eating. The vines climb high into the birch trees. Years ago they were kept trimmed and reachable. They are planted along the base of the stone wall that once divided the pasture from the orchard. The great mass of stones kept them warm.

We got home ahead of the rain and built a huge fire in the fireplace. The wind was almost a gale.

OCTOBER 15

A windy, cool, sunny, beautiful day. I stacked wood in the morning and then drove Lorna to the airport, did errands in Augusta and Waterville. Rain late afternoon and evening, with high wind. Watched Foreman pound Dino Dennis and Roberto Duran win in round one, and Mondale look decent and say little against Dole, who looked ugly, lied, sloganeered. Wonderful debate!

OCTOBER 16

Bright and windy and cool. The white maple deep magenta leaves are down. There are still the oranges and yellows of the birches, poplars, and a few maples, but the white trunks of birches stand out now on the near hills, and the gray criss-crossing of trunks and branches dulls the hills considerably and begins the cold bleak look we'll have from the end of October to the first snow.

We hear of snow already in northern Maine.

I stacked and split wood for three hours at the cabin. Garden work later in the afternoon.

OCTOBER 17—SUNDAY

Bright, cool, windy. George Blodgett came with his cordwood saw and a friend, and the three of us cut ten cords of wood in five hours. After they left, I split half a cord and carted it to the woodshed in the garden cart, and stacked it—a twelve-hour day, very tired, but it felt good.

OCTOBER 19

Gorgeous fall day, too beautiful to do anything, absolutely lazy. Some target shooting with the pistol. I'm not experienced enough to be consistent, but some of my shots are surprising. A partridge flew over while I was shooting. I spent an hour and a half stalking slowly through the crunching woods—stopping every ten yards and listening. Not far from the cabin I had a clear ground shot at a huge partridge—and missed.

I had intended to stay at the cabin, but I decided to go down and see how the kids were doing. Mabel had left Susie in charge of the house and gone off to a school meeting, taking Michael. I stayed and read to them.

OCTOBER 20

Heavy rain, beginning in the night. Came and went all day, sometimes a drizzle.

I drove to Augusta to have work done on the car, and then had a couple of hours of talk and booze with Herb Hartman, whom I met years ago skiing at Enchanted Mountain, and who's now director of Maine's Department of Parks and Recreation. He's a great hiker, climber, canoeist, translator of French poetry (though he hasn't done any for several years).

It was a good visit, city-country talk, and woods tales, and talk of McPhee's pieces in *The New Yorker* on trips down the Allegash and the making of birchbark canoes. Herb had sent me the pieces the week before.

OCTOBER 21

Rain heavier and rained all night. The lower road is severely flooded, not only from the outlet of the pond, but directly from the pond itself, the beaver dams have raised the level so high.

Susie hiked to school through the woods, with her yellow raincoat and orange knapsack—very chipper.

Quayle, four years old, had stayed with Becky the night before, and she and Becky and Michael were playing. Mabel said, "It's nice how the kids remember the problems of two years younger. Becky saw that Quayle had her right shoe on her left foot, and helped her. And Quayle sees that Michael is trying to pull up his pants but can't, because he's standing on the end. She probably remembers doing that."

When the rain let up, I walked Becky and Quayle to school through the woods, stopping at "Amy's Barn" to let Quayle's mother put dry shoes on her. I called the game warden while she was doing this, since only the wardens are allowed to dynamite the beaver dams. And she called the phone company to report that our phone was out of order. But walking up the hill like this is no longer a pleasant trip, since the barn is full of people (five) I don't like and scarcely know.

The warden had said, "Do you want to break the dam? Go ahead, I give you permission." I knew that he knew that those things are almost impossible to break short of dynamiting them—but I thought I might cut a notch or channel and expedite the drying of the road. So I took an axe, bar, spade, mattock and went down to look at the dams. Ha! They themselves were under two feet of water.

After supper I drove to the edge of the flood and walked on through it with rubber boots up to Ted's house. He leaves in two days on a reading tour that will take him finally to San Miguel, New Mexico, where he's rented a house and will stay for six months. Jake and Alison will drive out in a month and join him.

We "bitched the universe," but also listened to Haydn's 22nd Symphony, which Ted especially likes. He sorted over seeds to take with him, since he'll plant a garden as soon as he arrives.

The music room is filled with records now—all of Mozart, all of Beethoven, all of Haydn, all of Mahler. The Haydn symphonies—104 of them—had just arrived a few days ago.

In spite of our bad quarrels I still like Ted and feel more akin to him than to anyone else in Temple—though I can't stomach his poet chums. Instead of our semi-annual fight, round one of which is usually an attack-defense of Ezra Pound, I borrowed Kenner's book on Pound from him.

Tammy and Steve will stay in the house while Ted and Alison are gone. Ted is locking the music room and putting the valuable books in hiding.

OCTOBER 22

The hills now are green and orange—the latter being a few young maple, a few birches, and quite a few poplars. But the great mass of maple color has "gone by," as they say here, and the evergreens are dominant again—except in the rare places where there are stands of oak. The oak leaves are still intact, a dark leathery brown, with faint washes of orange and green. The hill beyond the Kimbers has some.

I'll spend the evening with Dick Blodgett, re-scoring the Ali-Norton fight, which Norton really won; and then watching the Carter-Ford bout, less interesting.

OCTOBER 23

A dusting of snow everywhere, dripping eaves, and vapors rising from the roofs as the sun strikes them.

I scored the fight 9-5-1 for Norton. The last Frazier fight seems to have taken a lot out of Ali. He didn't look good, spirit low.

Mabel joined us to watch Carter-Ford.

Susie was entertaining four chums, including Nellie, so Becky was happy. They twitter and screech like a flock of birds, run everywhere, and have such a marvelous good time as is hard for adults to even imagine.

OCTOBER 26

Snow on the hilltop; cold and windy. There are still some leaves on the poplars, beeches, and maple saplings, and oaks, but the hills have the massive dark color of evergreen hills.

I went to Eddie's to get the axe handles, hammer handles, and maul handles he had made for us. His little workshop is a pleasant place, jammed full of machines and wood, finished handles, unfinished handles. Often, in the little heated cubicle, there are violins in different stages. An Aladdin kerosene heater, coffee pot on top of it, his own fiddle, his cassette tape machine and dozens of cassettes of country music, fiddle music he's recorded himself, going around to friends and neighbors who have collections of it, or are fond of it and have old 78's from years and years ago. There were at least eighty cassettes stored in plastic bags—I suppose to keep the sawdust off them. He looked through most of them, searching for one he wanted me to hear. He said he had sold the violin he had made out of popple. His nephew had brought up a country-music fiddler to see him, a man who'd been playing forty-three years, and he had fallen in love with the popple fiddle. "I recorded it, it's right here somewhere." He put it on. Nellie had come into the little cubicle with us and we all three listened to it. "He can draw the sound out of a fiddle," Eddie said. "He's an Indian," Nellie said. "Part," said Eddie, "he's a man with a moustache—did you ever see whiskers on an Indian?"

The fiddle music was incredibly vigorous and piercing—it made you want to dance. "That's his foot tapping," said Eddie, "and that other sound is my nephew moving his beer bottle on the table."

"Oh yes," said Nellie, "he moved his beer bottle! *Didn't* he! *My Lord!*" A thick voice on the cassette said, "Go Evan! Yeah! Yeah!" And another voice a little later—it was Eddie's—said, "Now I hear you!"

I asked Eddie if he still fiddled himself and he said, "Oh, sometimes." The fiddler on the cassette was playing double strings and plucking, all very very fast. "If Eddie tried *that* he'd get tied up in knots," said Nellie. She used to play the piano with him when they played for country dances years ago. He'd start off by asking her, "What gear are we in?"

We talked a bit about fiddle makers. Eddie had heard of a young woman in Maine who made them, and also of a sea captain on the coast who gets $500 apiece for his. The popple fiddle was sold for $150. I asked him if he needed any more broken glass—which he uses to shave and shape the thin sounding boards that form the backs and fronts of the fiddles. I told him we had a good supply of it, since Sashka, our malamute, has broken three or four windows when we've made the mistake of locking her in the house.

Eddie insisted that I take one axe handle free, in exchange for the big butt piece of white ash I'd brought him last year. His handles are far stronger than "boughten" ones, "because they're split from the wood, not sawed from it," he says. He thinks the kiln-dried wood is brittle, too, where the air-dried wood is not. They have a good feel to them, and they *do* last longer.

There was a massive maul leaning against the wall. "That's a sixteen pounder," he said, "that's not for splitting wood. I used it to break rocks with. The last time I used that was when I was widening the cellar in Slim Hodgkin's old house. There were some boulders there as big as that snow-thrower (he pointed to the machine in the corner). I used that to break them up with . . . well . . . I could handle it. . . ."

Eddie has had three heart attacks, and is supposed to be dieting, but his weight is over two hundred again, though he's not any taller than five-eight. His shoulders, neck, and chest are massive. His skull and jaw are rounded and boney. Nellie had a serious heart attack last year, and she too is supposed to be dieting, but she's as round and hefty as ever—maybe five-one.

I noticed the transformer for an electric fence hanging on the wall and asked what it was for. "Keep the coons out of the garden," he said. "They don't like to have their noses burnt." He nodded toward the garden right outside the window. I asked how many strands there were. "At first there was just one," he said, "about eight inches off the ground, but the coons jumped over it. So I put another strand on, and that kept the coons out, but one day Leo Rieu's cows got loose and they stepped right over the second strand, so I put a third one . . . ."

"They wandered quite a way," I said. "*Didn't* they!" said Nellie (she actually almost screams these things; her voice is both soft and shrill, with notes of hilarity and irony). "*Didn't* they! And *weren't* they *hungry!*"

"The only trouble with the electric fence," said Eddie, "is it kills the birds. They walk under it and touch their heads. . . ."

Nellie is immediately grave and sympathetic. She sucks in her breath and says, "Yes," sorrowfully.

They are like pioneers living at the edge of the wilderness, too much alone, but consciously maintaining certain amenities, working hard for them. Eddie is extremely resourceful—designs his own tools on occasion. An unusual man, actually. He can't read, but can write numbers. Nellie reads and writes for him. He went to work when he was twelve, after the death of his mother.

Giving me an axe handle in thanks for the butt of ash is typical of him. I thanked him, and he said, "You're welcome," with a formality and sweet graciousness one doesn't see much of these days, though other of the very old here have displayed it: Mark Mitchell and Walter McCoy (both dead), and of course Dana Hamlin.

Ice in the puddles before supper time, and a high wind. Sashka was frisky, ran in great, sharp-banking circles, and teased Shem. I threw the ball for Shem, and this made Sashka so jealous she was at him from all sides and confused him so that he didn't know where the ball had gone. I walked to the end of the long yard behind the house and picked it up, the dogs following me all the way, Sashka teasing Shem constantly and each trying to get closer to me than the other, stumbling against my legs repeatedly. I threw the ball back toward the front of the house, Shem went after it and Sashka after Shem, running figure eights around him as he lumbered straight ahead. Evening was coming on and there was just a hint of duskiness in the light. Just as the dogs caught up with the ball at the far end of the house, the two ponies emerged into view, running friskily at the dogs. Shem picked up the ball, and all four animals wheeled and ran toward me together, a beautiful and totally surprising sight.

The ponies seem huge and powerful, and are as furry as bears with their winter coats. Chin-Chin is like black velvet. I said to someone that we might move the ponies to Esther Johnson's pasture for hunting season. "You better. Chin-Chin will be shot for a bear and Starbright for a deer."

Another sign of winter: the glittering hoarfrost on the chin whiskers of the ponies.

OCTOBER 27

Wood splitting at cabin and house.

I had said I would do some literature with some of the kids from school (excluding the two teenage boys I can't stand)—but only if they'd come to the house. Amelia (almost fourteen—very pretty, very smart) and Cindy (almost fifteen, earnest but confused and vague) walked through the woods and showed up a half hour late. I'd spent a couple of hours preparing a "lesson" (a presentation, *something*—poetry shouldn't be *taught)* on ballads, old and new. We read several of the famous old ones, plus Keats's "La Belle Dame Sans Merci"—plus Lorca's "*Verde que te quiero verde . . .*" in a marvelous translation that was in *American Poetry Review.*

But the session was flat, not interesting to me, or meaningful. Cindy could just as well be reading detective stories (I don't feel that quality "takes" with her). Amelia could do it by herself with a reading list and occasional consultation. Maybe I'll put it on that basis for all of them. That way only those who are strongly and especially interested will come to me.

Back to the woodpile after they left.

At night, after supper, Mabel, Michael, and Becky took a bath together. A constant chattering came from the bathroom—joking, complaining, chattering, with much laughter, Becky especially, laughing throatily like Mabel. In some important way these are Mabel's preferred companions. Her voice behind the closed door was just like theirs.

She came out. Becky and Michael stayed in the water. He was pouring water over her from a sprinkling can.

Mabel and Michael went to a meeting at school. I read a long while to Becky. Susie was visiting friends. When Mabel came back she had runaway Shem with her, but he didn't follow her into the house, he stayed in the car. After a while I went out to get him. He was in the back seat. I opened the door and called him. He didn't come, just looked at me in his mopish way. I called several times, then I went around and opened the other door, nearer him, thinking I'd pull him out if he didn't come. I called him one more time, somewhat angrily, and this time he responded. I started back to the house. Sashka was running around him trying to provoke him into play, but he wasn't responding to her. I looked back and saw that he was limping badly. I went back to him and looked at the front leg he was favoring. The skin was hanging open—like a large tear in someone's pant leg—and the pale red meat was visible for at least two inches up and down, and an inch across. The tear was sharp, not jagged. (Mabel had noticed that he was limping, but she never is much interested in Shem—or other animals, or machinery—and she hadn't examined him.)

I put some merthiolate on the cut and bandaged it. Mabel took him to the vet in the morning. The vet said the gash was from barbed wire—not a bullet, as, for a while, we feared.

OCTOBER 28

Late in the afternoon I took soil samples from the downhill fields beside the house. The fat, frisky ponies saw and heard the bucket, and hoping that there were oats in it, came to look. They followed me all around the field, and then they decided it was time for their evening run. Starbright jumped in the air and kicked his heels, and they sped off downhill, headlong, first one leading, then the other. They wheeled, criss-crossed up the hill, circled the house, came down again and vanished into the woods.

As I walked back and forth gathering samples from the worn-out hillside field, I saw that the ponies' path had reestablished the old farm road, which used to come out of the woods and climb the hill in serpentine loops—horses pulling a wagon. The internal combustion engine has led to steep roads, right angle turns—a rectilinear imposition on a landscape that doesn't have *any* straight lines.

Slim's son and his wife have taken over the store, but Slim shows up there frequently. We talked about the terrible drop in the size of the deer herd. "It's because so many farms have gone back to woods," he said. "The deer liked the apples and the fields."

I'd read somewhere that the greatest density of deer is in New Jersey—many, many times that of Maine's one deer per square mile of forest. New Jersey has the greatest human density in the country too, and in fact three of its small cities are the most densely populated cities in the world—Weehawken, Union City, and the third may be Jersey City. The first two out-rank Shanghai and the cities of Holland. (There are *areas* in other cities that are far more dense than these.) But every year a couple of dozen hunters come up from New Jersey to their camps in Temple. Slim said, "Well, they like to get away."

OCTOBER 29

A mild fall day, mild wind, mild sun. Things close seem bright, but the hills three miles away have the look of being seen through a faint haze of smoke, or through glass partly darkened by smoke. There are large smoke-dark clouds in the west, but between these clouds, and in the east, where the clouds are whiter, the sky is blue.

I owe Bob Kimber several hours of work. I went down there in the afternoon to help Bob, Rita, Sandy, and Susan move the firewood into the shed. Bob and Rita—who may translate my children's book into German—have been going to Portland several times a week for almost a year for the dialysis Rita needs after her kidney disease. But they were trained there in the use of the machine and now have one at home. Rita had spent four hours that morning hooked up to the machine. Susan is living with them, with her child Terra, because she has broken up with Norman, who sleeps regularly with Christine.

Christine still works at the dairy barn with Jack, who sleeps regularly with Michelle at Amy's barn, etc., etc., etc.

Bob's firewood—very neatly stacked under sheets of tin here and there in the yard—is not only old and dry, but is cut to stove length (eighteen inches) and is therefore quite light, especially compared to mine, which I'd spent the morning splitting—green oak, rock maple, etc., cut in two-foot lengths and quite heavy. Bob had borrowed a truck and we loaded, unloaded, and stacked the wood in the shed, quickly and very cheerfully, with me cracking jokes and occasionally figuring out how Laurel and Hardy would handle things.

I noticed Bob's old-fashioned high-topped boots (army boots, but quite old) and said they reminded me of Dana Hamlin's shoes. Dana is 95 now and lives on a nearby farm with several other old men. I saw him at the bank half a year ago, so sweet and cheerful, his thumb and forefinger poking curiously into a tiny snap-shut change purse. He was wearing high-top black shoes with round toes and soft, soft leather, the soles no thicker than an eighth of an inch. Bob and Rita bought his old farm when he grew too old to manage it. He loved the place and has been pleased that they've done so well with it, and keep sheep and chickens, like he did. Bob says he comes to see them at least twice a year. They're fond of him. Everyone is. He's a serene, sweet-natured man, at peace with the world and apparently totally accepting of himself. Bob says that in the last few years he has failed a lot, but still has an astonishing memory, and says things like, "on June 6, 1933 . . ." or "that was February of '58 . . ."—talking about weather, prices, old county fairs. I don't know how many children he has. One son is almost 70. Several years ago he came up on our hill here with his sister—at least five years older than he, a frail, small, wrinkled woman who had to be helped from the car, but whose face was still bright with intelligence. She wanted to see the view once again. It was a place she knew well from her youth. Now all his brothers and sisters are dead. And I remember thinking at the time that there aren't many places in the United States where anyone can look at the landscape of his youth.

While I worked at Bob's, Chuck worked here, hauling and stacking wood that I'd split. When I talk with all these exiles from the cities I hear the Maine accents and the localisms coming into their voices. I hear these things in my own: I say *ayeh* sometimes, and often mutter to myself at the end of a sentence *yeh, mm, mm-hmm,* affirming it. I heard Bob mutter this way, and Chuck and Leon. And when I read the *Little House* books to Becky, I recognize the humor that is distinctly country humor, as when the cat confounds the attacking dog by jumping on its back and digging in its claws; the dog runs howling with the cat on its back, and then "when Kitty figured she was far enough from home she thanked him and jumped off." (Actually, I threw in the "thanked him"—which is salty-dog country, not plain country.)

There is so much wordless activity in country life, so much being alone, so much physical work that does actually succeed in important close ways (the wood pile, the garden—both of which can be very handsome, very satisfying to look at, as well as necessary to have), and the people are busy, busy, busy here, but are not distracted—and there is something genuinely supportive and consoling in the great beauty of the natural world—all of this has to show up in the speech, to say nothing of the specific effects of the farming vocabulary and attitudes: "gone by," "used up," "winter never rots in the sky."

Susie spent her first few years in New York. Her speech is like that of the other "new arrivals." But Becky is a country girl. Her voice is louder and more energetic than Susie's, much broader (to accomodate the tones that express feeling; whereas Susie's is slurred and rapid, more "intellectual") and Becky goes to the *stow-ah,* and loves to go sled-riding in the *wintuh.*

After working at Bob's, I split some more wood at home. Just before supper Susie was playing music on the phonograph. Michael began to dance, as he often does, not just twirling and stomping, but really dancing, using arms and head and inventing gestures. His expression, his whole attitude is *rapt.* (This may come from the Bread and Puppet tour—hearing so much music and seeing so much theater and dance before the age of two.) I was watching him. He noticed it. I smiled at him—and this was enough to ruin it for him. He stopped dancing. Mabel was hurt and said, "You shouldn't smile at him when he's dancing." She's right. My approval can only be destructive in this kind of thing. It invades the activity perhaps even more than disapproval would. The only correct thing—as Mabel said—is to leave the child alone.

The image of that tiny creature dancing is the best symbol I know of for the I-Thou of the child's world. One must learn to distinguish this from other activities that resemble it. Help those others—but leave this one alone.

That evening I drove Becky and Susie to the Halloween party at the Sandy River School. Becky was partly in costume (a baby—she had pads on her knees for crawling, a nursing bottle in one hand), Susie planned to make up as a clown when she got there. Michael wanted to come. He had a satchel full of something or other. We brought him along, and fortunately he fell asleep, as it would have been impossible to get him to leave the party.

I carried in a bag of goodies sent by Mabel. Several of the girls were putting on costumes in the little kitchen when I opened the door. Pretty Amelia, almost fourteen, was naked to the waist. Her breasts are fully formed and beautiful. That pale white, very white, but healthy skin was smoother and more glowing than I remembered skin could be. She was partly embarrassed, partly proud. I ducked out quickly. What a vision!

I stopped at the Kimbers' to pick up a bottle of bourbon they'd bought for us, and I opened it there and sat drinking awhile with Bob and Rita.

While reading ballads with Amelia and Cindy a few days ago I came on the phrase "middle earth," which meant this earth, but experienced as a place beneath heaven and above hell. And then a few days later I felt one of those flashes of intuition: how vivid and immediate life must have been when people lived in "middle earth," were accountable and knew they'd die. I spoke of all this with the Kimbers; and said that it was striking that present-day followers of religious leaders like Moon, or the Transcendental Meditators, or the dozens of others, never defend their faith with reason, but only with a demonstration of faith: smiling, nodding, affirming it; whereas in the real ages of faith, men defended their belief with vigorous applications of reason.

And then home: the whiskey was for a small meeting of parents who are much displeased with the school, especially with Tim, the teacher, who is probably a borderline psychotic, extremely anxious, out of touch, capable of serious breakdown. Luanne is not bad for the younger kids, but for my money is a dreadful kind of person, a suburban tea-party, life is beautiful, anti-violence kind of person who takes all the spontaneity out of life and all the emotion.

We drank the bourbon. It was pleasant for a while. Leon and Mary came, Ann Van der Weile, Mimi Brennan. But the more I heard about the school the more upset I became. And the problem of coping with Jack Carson, whom I do detest; and all the drugs at Amy's barn in her absence, and . . . Boring to think about, all of it, but very upsetting. I'm surrounded by people I can't stand and who are close enough, both physically and in terms of activity, to grate against me, upset me, poison my very susceptible thoughts. *All* are in this position because of Mabel's charity. If her charity were utterly removed, none of them would be here, including Jack Carson, and the place would be much better for me.

I went up to the cabin a little drunk and very angry. And so the meeting used up not only Friday night, but most of Saturday as well, because I couldn't sleep, and seriously wondered if I should take an apartment in Portland and spend alternate weeks here with Mabel and the kids. I can't control this environment even a little, whereas if I lived alone I could at least free myself of these dreadful counter-culture culture-less people, these Tims, and Jacks, and Dick Coopers, and the whole wretched crew whom I know because they know Mabel.

Though—to be fair—it's Mabel *plus* the needs of the children that have led to this.

It was a dazzlingly pretty night, walking up to the cabin, the stars very very sharp, the sky actually sparkling, Jupiter large and bright, Sirius brilliant—and bare branches of the trees standing out against it.

OCTOBER 30

Since I only slept about two hours and wanted to sleep more and couldn't, I went down to the house and split wood until I got really tired. Mabel was getting ready to feed and sleep an itinerant group of singers who were performing in Farmington that night, and with whom her good friend Trudi sometimes performs. I slept until 10:30 P.M., and went down to the house after 11:00. They were all in the big room, plus Charlie Adams, stoned as always, plus Dick Cooper; and the singers were *not* attractive. I filled a plate with food, took a glass of wine and went upstairs. Then back to the cabin.

OCTOBER 31—SUNDAY

Writing and painting at the cabin, heavy day-long rain and fog, November weather, but a good fire in the stove, and peace.

Looked at Aragon's sumptuous two volumes on Matisse. The illustrations wonderful and the text absurdly conceited, conceited as only the French can manage, and quite worthless as well. But the paintings! Also looked at a lot of de Kooning—and then did some pastels.

Alison and Jake are coming to supper, then all the kids will go trick-or-treating—if the rain isn't too heavy.

The rain stopped at suppertime. I started the generator on the way down. The kids met me at the door. The big room was dark, three shining Jack-o-lanterns stood on the table, and there was a pleasant scent of burning pumpkin. Jake and Alison were there, and Jake rushed around to show me his mask, his candy bag. I asked Alison if Mabel had offered her a job as a free school teacher. She said, "Is one available?" (She would be good at it, she's *real,* and smart, and firm.) Mabel came in while I was mentioning the shortcomings of the teachers, and said in an accusatory way how pleasant the house had been that morning with the twelve guests; and I said my cabin had been pleasant too, and there was no reason why we shouldn't do things that way . . . but I went on to say I couldn't stand talking with Dick Cooper, or Charlie, and perhaps I started to rail, which she made worse by saying that maybe I should join co-counselling as it might lead to a more positive attitude toward the people around me; and I said my detestation of them *was* a positive attitude . . . and worse *and* worse, all in five minutes. I apologized to Alison and went back to the cabin, again too upset to work.

I'm not really angry at Mabel. The situation as a whole is simply not good for me. I'm thinking seriously now of getting a place in Portland and coming here on alternate weekends.

NOVEMBER 1

—So. I missed seeing the kids in their Halloween costumes. Mabel had made a cat costume for Becky, but Becky wouldn't wear it, and dressed up as a gypsy. Susie dressed as a clown. Jake, dressed as a monkey, went with them.

On the way to the house yesterday, before the quarrel, I stopped on the road to jot in my notebook: wet leaves on the road, tree trunks and branches almost black in the rain, but the brilliant pale leaves of the little beech trees stand out vividly, spear-shaped, fish-shaped, their color a pale mix of ivory, saffron, salmon, but pale and bright, getting paler and more vivid day by day. They look like they should be transparent, but they aren't.

Tonight there's snow in the wind, "spitting snow." And there was a Sasquatch bootprint in the mud of the road: Shem's broad paw overlay a print of my boot, and the claws fell exactly where my toes would be if they showed through the boot.

NOVEMBER 8

A threatening squall.

It's windy and the sky is overcast, except in the northwest (Mount Blue) and there a pale buttermilk haze, a *chunk* of haze, covers the tops of the hills and moves towards us, covering the slopes and then the tops of the next hills, and then *those* slopes. The wind abates noticeably. There are a few skittering snowflakes in the air, large and light.

In the east—straight opposite all this—the sky is bright blue with huge clouds that are both gray and white. Suddenly the air is dancing with snowflakes and the wind is blowing hard. But now a patch of blue opens directly west, as if a bright blue wedge had been driven into the buttermilk squall. The blue sky grows wider, the hills reappear, the dancing snowflakes are gone.

The squall, quite small, now moves away up the next-but-one north-north-east valley. Its southern member dissipates.

NOVEMBER 11

Another sign of approaching winter, hard winter: the ground is suddenly strange underfoot, unyielding. All the ruts and little mud ridges of the preceding wet weeks at the end of October—the ridges around boot prints, tire tracks, and the little mounds kicked up by the sharp hooves of the ponies—all these that used to yield slowly under the weight of one's foot, now support the foot or deflect it, so that walking is suddenly awkward.

Constant wind for days. The ice in the puddles doesn't melt anymore, but the little stream that passes under the cabin road is still bubbling and flowing. Large rocks near the surface of the earth seem to have sunk a little deeper. The earth around them has frozen and lifted a bit so that a tracing of air-space outlines each stone.

NOVEMBER 13

After so many gray days, a blue and bright one, windy but not raw, so pleasant to be out in that I gathered dead wood and sawed it for the cabin stove.

The woods are full of hunters. I used to worry about Shem getting shot, and once searched for him in the woods, calling anxiously. Now he must take his chances. I say to myself, "I hope they don't shoot him."

NOVEMBER 14—SUNDAY

No hunting allowed on Sunday—good, because both dogs ran off through the woods to Porter Hill.

Not a pretty day, but a very pleasant one, the air brisk and delicious to breathe, as if it came to us over snowfields. In the early afternoon I walked into the woods toward Porter Hill and fell into a wood-management reverie, mentally marking the trees to be cut and cleared. A lot of snow-damaged gray birch in there that would be good to get rid of. As I looked this way and that, I saw a tiny sand-colored moth beating its way among the leafless trees. I wondered where it was going, and by what method, and what it would do when it got there. How could it survive the freezing nights?

I went on up the path, and suddenly there ahead of me, strolling companionably through the woods, were Shem and Sashka. They ran to meet me. We went on up the hill together. Later, when I returned to the cabin, they went on down to the house.

And I saw another of the little moths.

NOVEMBER 15

There are ribbons of permanent ice now at the edges of the streams. Snowflakes in the air for several days, but no snowfall. Vermont, New Hampshire, and northern Maine all have snow.

It was a poor year for apples. No one wanted to make cider.

NOVEMBER 18

The pine tree outside my cabin door looks freshly green. Its straw colored needles from last year fell with the falling of the other leaves—but now it has all this new green instead of bare branches.

Alison had dinner with us last night. She leaves Saturday to drive across the country (Jeannie will go with her) and join Ted in New Mexico.

JANUARY 18

Weeks of zero weather, occasionally a bit below, only once or twice much above. Good snow cover now—about two feet—and I've had several good (short) ski outings.

Generator kaput, living with kerosene lamps, a nuisance in this big house.

> *Snowflakes*
> *are streaming by the window,*
> *the turbulence lifts one*
> *and holds it there*
> *then that one too*
> *flies by.*

> *A high wind in spring*
> *scoops a leaf from the ground*
> *and hurls it upward*
> *in a smooth, flat curve*
> *drops weightily on the branch of a tree*
> *revealed   as   a   bird.*

[NEIGHBORS]

Oiva Ansden

Walked some of our lines with Oiva Ansden, half brother of Vilio.

"I got this land—this and the other piece—from Maury Jessup just before he went back to Finland, back to the old country, you know. He give it to me almost for nothing. He cut it over clean. Same with the other piece. Anything that could go to the mill he took."

I: "Do you want to leave it to your children?"

Oiva: "I don't have any children. I been shootin' blanks all my life. That's what a fellow said to me once.

"No, I promised Hutchins he could have first refusal on this, I wouldn't want to go back on that.

"Here, here's my corner right here—it goes up along that stone wall . . . that's a funny angle, isn't it? Look how it jogs off there . . . then it goes on north and out to that little pond, then down back along the stream to the bridge down here . . . it's out now . . . and then back here.

"When I got the lower piece I wasn't sure where the line was, but I knew it was up against a piece belonged to Richard Blodgett, and I knew he'd know the line . . . well I knew he would, he was brought up here, and he and Jules cut a lot of pine right up the hill there. Oh, that was a pretty stand of pine. He took me right to the corner up here and we found that barb wire fence . . . and Jules walked the other line . . . that was hard to find, it wasn't on posts or trees like here, it was layin' on the ground, you had to hunt for it. But we met right up there at the point. It's a pie-shaped piece. It's forty acres, but it looks bigger. Now here's where it jogs down and crosses the road. Do you know Malcolm Peters—well he's the surveyor here in Farmington. When he did Hutchins' lines I asked him to do mine on this side. This is his pipe here, and then it's that stone wall by the big yellow birches. It goes right in to the pond. He told me it's a good idea to drive in a smaller pipe first, drive it all the way in, then put this bigger pipe right over it and drive *that* in. Then if anybody moves the big pipe a few yards away, you know . . . there might be some good trees in there . . . you can always dig around and find that little pipe in the ground.

"I went to school from the old French place up there on the land you bought from Hoxie. The shell of the house must still be standing. I wasn't born there, I was born in New Jersey, but my folks split up and my mother married again . . . that was Vilio's father . . . I was about four when we lived here, and then I went to school right down here in the little red school house. I couldn't speak a word of English, only Finnish. But there were a lot of Finns here then, a whole lot. I just picked it up as I went along.

"No, I hated farming. I milked the cows as soon as I was big enough to sit on one of those little stools. No, what I wanted to do was drive a truck, and first chance I got, I did. I drove for several years, then I drove a bus four years, then I worked as a mechanic out at Morton Motors. I went to World War II, I was overseas two years . . . Vilio was in Iceland and Europe, but I went the other way, I was in the Pacific . . . I was in three years and six months all together. I knew my job would be waitin' for me, that was government regulations, you know, they had to hold your job for you . . . but Bob Hartley was in there then and I said, 'My job open?' I knew it was, I knew they had to keep it open for me, and he said, 'Sure, you can sign up on the GI Bill,' and I said, 'No sir, I ain't signin' no more papers for Uncle Sam,' and I walked out right then and there. He wanted me to sign on as apprentice—after workin' there eight years. That way the government could pay two-thirds. No, sir.

"We lived up the Day Mountain road then. You know where Jeb Ellis is? We had a farm right back in there. Frank Searles told me there was a job with the mechanic, and I went right to work the next morning.

"My cousin's going to help me cut up this wood and haul it. I'm not supposed to use a chain saw or lift anything. No, it's not my back. I was in the hospital last year . . . when I came to, they told me that they cut out eighty percent of my stomach. That was the worst blow I ever had in my life. I worked for years at Knowlton McLeary, had a good job there, good pay and all the overtime I wanted, and I was workin' for my retirement . . . well . . . I had to let it go, it was lifting, you know . . . I got a hernia soon enough anyway. . . ."

A lean man of middle height, sixty-five but looks older. Injury or deformity on lower lip, a lot of scar tissue on the lip itself. Shy, decent. Set off into the woods walking fast, as people do here in order to get the thing done. Carried an axe—"I like to take an axe when I go in the woods." Now and then cut a tree sprout; put a blaze mark on a boundary tree.

Wore a red hat of waterproof plastic material, popular here; a quilted gray vest—like a down vest, but some sort of fiber-fill. People use them in the woods. Eyeglasses.

DANA HAMLIN

"Won't somebody help me. Help me. Won't somebody tell me what my trouble is. Won't somebody help me." Loud, chanted; a wailing yet droning tone desperate but boring, clear to everyone that there was no immediate emergency. Thin, wild-eyed, white-haired, powdery white skin, bluish cast to the skin of the thighs where her hospital gown had risen. A large doll on the tray of her wheelchair. She holds a diaper by one corner, trailing it on the floor, flapping it feebly toward whoever looks at her. This chanting broke in on us toward the end of the hour. It was eerie, broke my attention to Dana. I wheeled him out to the community room when I left and saw her. When I arrived, an hour earlier, she was quiet, was stroking the head of the doll that lay across the tray. She wasn't stroking it vaguely, but with firm contact and the kind of pause in the stroke that would serve to catch the baby's hair (if it had been a baby) and brush it away from the eyes.

Dana in the wheelchair, looking down, gathering his thoughts. One can see the huge function of energy. More is there than he can easily obtain for articulate memory—and if the whole thing can be energized, it will come out. That is what he seems to be trying to do.

To see the faculties dying, tissue dying, is to realize what a miraculous creation these sentient tissues are.

When I came to the nursing home yesterday: garish color TV, shrieking fat woman, palsied man making grotesque faces like a blow fish, "What can I do for you? What can, etc.?" rapidly—a scene of craziness and fragmentation, not age. Dana sane and rational in this madhouse of old age. Dana was sitting at the table (an empty table) in his wheelchair, sleeping, body collapsed inward on itself, his head dangling down like the head of a sunflower that has ripened and the frost has killed it, and now, on an upright stalk, the drooping head looks straight down, staring, full face into the earth. I talked to the cheerful young woman in the tiny cubicle of the office. She told me two o'clock would be a good time to talk with him. I drove around the Mosher Hill area, beautiful vistas, my fall feeling of nostalgia, *déjà vu,* and longing. A light rain—dry places on the road under the big trees.

The *cheerful, giving* character of the young women nurses.

"Can you bring me a glass of water?" "Sure can."—brisk, cheerful, comes almost at a run. This is by no means a common or much-encountered temperament, but it seems to me to be a rural and maybe a state of Maine temperament and I love it. Dana such a sweet *good* person. I wanted to caress his cheek, kiss him when I left—everything sweet and dear about age, all the power and fearsomeness taken away and that long experience of the world couched there almost as in an infant's body. I did pat his back; we are really strangers. And yet we began talking about Temple when I arrived. He didn't know me, didn't remember the two brief encounters we'd had. I appeared in his field of vision wanting to talk about Temple, and so he talked about Temple. The mere process of establishing where I lived resurrected the remembered places and turns of his milk route, and he began to talk—though with difficulty. Never asked my name, but wanted me to please repeat where it was I lived.

Dana answered questions that I hadn't yet put into words and that actually changed, or seemed to change, the drift of our talk. Like a child. I could believe in some sort of clairvoyance—so little static of self.

Dick Blodgett: "It's amazing he's still alive. He's been in more accidents and had more broken bones. Horses ran away with him, pulled him all over the place. And when they bulldozed the dump, once he backed up with a load of garbage and went right over."

Born 1880.

"I hauled milk for sixty years. That's a long time. I believe I've gone more miles on a milk route than any man in the world.

"The old creamery failed, so my dad went around to the farmers and asked if they'd let us haul their cream down to the North Turner creamery. They said they would. It was March. My dad took ill and my brother was shearing sheep, so dad said to me would you rather haul milk or shear? and I said it didn't make any difference, both o' them was work. So that's when I started. I was sixteen years old."

When Dana said "both o' them was work," a light of wit came to his face—remarkable to see this. His sweet smile and a brightening of the watery left eye.

Handkerchief in his breast pocket. He extracts it with a certain effort and deliberation. He had already said to me, "I can only see out of this eye. This one here has cataracts. I could have had 'em taken off. Maybe I should've, but my sister did, and she had a bad time with it."

Now he said, "My eyes water an awful lot." He held the handkerchief to his eye repeatedly, not dabbing, but holding it there, as if letting it soak up the fluid.

"When this leg gets better, I'll send for my crutches. My grandson has them. It would be easier for me to walk to the sitting room than turn these wheels."

About coming back. "We eat at around five, then pretty soon after, I start getting ready for bed. Yes, two o'clock is a good time."

Just before leaving, I explained to him why I had come in the first place. He said, "Well, I don't know what good I'll do, but I'll try to help." Seemed pleased.

I saw him at Temple's 175th anniversary party, sitting in his wheelchair in the back of the pickup truck. "My grandson laid two planks against the back o' the carriage and wheeled me right up. I could see everything. I sat just as close as I am to you to the tailgate of the carriage. More than a hundred people came by and talked to me."

I had seen him three years ago at the bank in Farmington, looking to the left and right with shy pleasure, a public figure, the oldest man, and so attractive in his pleased awareness of things that many did smile at him, so shy yet at ease—the grandfather of the town—anyone could greet him and he would greet anyone with a smile. Dipping into the little snap-purse, a leather pouch. His soft, button-up shoes, with their thin soles (like a dancer's slippers) were of the same vintage. He was walking well, and must have weighed twenty or thirty pounds more than he does now. He seems collapsed and desiccated. His arms are too weak to push the wheels of the wheelchair. His hands are misshapen, huge knuckles, fingers somewhat awry. They lie in his lap, a collection of bones in little bags of skin. He wears an old flannel shirt, checkered, and the dark green cotton work pants that farmers, mechanics, mill hands, woodcutters, etc. all wear around here. There is no meat on his shoulders or around his chest. Inside his shirt there is a cage of bones, and in that cage his heart is still beating. His hips seem wide and boney. His knees are boney, and there is nothing but bone between them and his hips, or between knees and feet. His neck is thin and weak, with loose seams and flaps of dusty soft skin; his head tilts forward. Bald, with a few dry strands of dead grass and broken spider webs this way and that, a little hair, cut short, above his ears. Pale, powdery, faintly speckled skin, a pale wart or cyst high in the middle of his forehead. Sunken temples. His ears seem large and protrude somewhat. Pale bristles of his eyebrows he scratches occasionally with his thumbnail, especially when he forgets something, and says, "Oh . . . it's funny . . . you know I can't always think of what I want to. Tell me again where you live." Prominent cheekbones, separated from his small, square jaw by deep creases and soft small folds of skin, his small nose, shrunken cartilege, a little button nose. Wide expressive mouth that smiles widely, upturned innocently at the corners like the smile of an introspective young child who is happy but does not grin. He talked for ten minutes or so, and then, "You know, I have some false teeth. I believe I could talk better if I put them in." He extracted them from the pocket of the flannel shirt where they were wedged behind a folded handkerchief, and with deliberate, somewhat tremulous movements fixed them (uppers) into place. "They drop out very easily now, so I keep them in my pocket. I lost two teeth out of them. I'm afraid of losing the whole thing." Said this with a brightening smile, attractive gentle humor. This was his first such sign of life. His voice is slow, hesitant, faint, but his sentences hang together, get finished, and go right ahead. So much effort goes into the mere act of talking, and of remembering, that often I thought he had lost the train of thought, or was even on the verge of nodding off into sleep—and though he did occasionally lose the thread, he surprised me again and again. "Mustache" of small, vertical wrinkles.

"I had four brothers, two sisters, and a mother and father—now I'm all that's left."

Dick Blodgett: "Dana's wife was the Sunday school teacher here in the Intervale. I went every Sunday. I was the only boy that did. (Laughs) Maybe that's why. She was a nice old lady."

DANA HAMLIN II

They were playing beano when I came, a more rational scene. The woman with the doll was off to one end by herself, not playing—and in Dana's room two old men were in bed, one trembling. ("How are you today?" "I'm all right." "Are you cold?" "Yes. I'm cold."—she covers him.)

I talk with Leon about permission and advisability of taking Dana for a ride. He likes the idea. Terrible difficulty of doing anything—extracting his handkerchief from his breast pocket, wiping his nose. He asked me to open the drawer. I helped rummage for his glasses. He checked the case. "I can't see out of one eye so I just have the one lens. Hah! I've got a cataract on my right eye. If I'd've had my wits about me, I'd've had it taken off years ago, but my sister had that operation and it gave her a lot of trouble and that discouraged me."

Life is reduced to a few things; each one is difficult, and is done slowly, with weak, trembling hands that are nothing but bone and tendon, knuckles, no meat, great hollows, great knobs, all speckled. Time goes very very slowly. Is it easier to face death this way—so far off, an hour is like three hours, or like a day—a long time between breakfast and dinner?

Hard to pick him up to help him pee in a plastic bottle. No weight in his legs. Leon: "He weighs 135, but it's all concentrated in the top. He's top-heavy. How's your back; it won't be easy getting him in and out of the car."

His large ears, the bald skin of head so pale, ivory thin, without blood. Everything sunken, collapsed, drawing near to the bone.

In the bed next to his, an old man on his back, mouth open, tongue sharp in position of pain, pointed nose aimed at the ceiling—death soon.

Helping him pee. "Hand me that bottle there. Now stand behind me and lift me up." When this is written down, it reads like ordinary speech, but each word is an effort, and there are no gestures, and the blind eye is expressionless and the other recessed in a small triangular aperture under a bristly, heavy white eyebrow. It was a task for his trembling fingers to open his pants, a task to locate his penis and get it into the mouth of the receptacle. And actually I thought he *hadn't,* that he had missed and would wet himself. I didn't know what to do, didn't want to embarrass him, and a small wetting would be no great consequence. But actually he had succeeded. His penis was so shrunken that I had thought part was hidden, bent under the edge of the plastic jar.

He wasn't entirely easy about the idea of driving with me, doesn't really know who I am, though he does really know where I live. "You go down that dirt road and take a right over the stream. There was some buildings set right up in there. That was the other Waltonen—yes, John. . . ."

Wears the ubiquitous dark green cotton work pants, now many many inches too large for him. A checked cotton work shirt, over that a dark gray solid color, medium weight cardigan sweater with black buttons. Brown corduroy bedroom slippers (he never leaves the wheelchair). Beside his bed are the old high-top shoes of soft, thin leather, thin soles, black, many eyelets for the laces. Another pair on a shelf in the closet. "Open that drawer"—a tone so gentle and so without ego that it doesn't even have the assertiveness of a request. In the drawer: a *National Geographic,* some bible pamphlets, a modest clutter. "I put my false teeth in that plastic cup at night." He wanted me to put it on top of the little bureau.

"Hoist me up." (Wanted to change to better pants. Get his purse, his gray felt hat, his gray suit coat. His glasses. Already had his teeth.)

We had begun talking in the community room just after the beano game. The visiting women began to lead the group (a dozen) in hymns. My loud voice was probably a nuisance (Dana a bit deaf, not bad though). I wheeled him back to his room.

The gaiety, a *tormented* gaiety, wild, bright-eyed, demented, of the sloppily fat woman—shrill bursts of laughter, little screams. An old white-haired woman whose knees touched when she walked, went outside, waved to me childishly from a bench when I left.

DANA HAMLIN III

Hunger for touch, like dying Jill, my dying mother—wants to kiss, be held. I saw this when Bob and Rita came to the car. He's fond of them, especially of Bob, who returns the affection, held Dana's hand, pressed his cheek to Dana's cheek, and Dana's face was *wreathed* (that word really fits: all that soft skin and those folds were lifted into arcs of smiles)—he nuzzled and kissed Bob's cheek. Same when Leon knelt at the front seat of the car, having helped me get Dana inside. Dana: "Aren't you coming?"

"I'd like to, but my boss would say no if I asked her. But I'd really like to. You'll have a good time." Dana's reactions were so ingenuous and childlike that there came a moment when Leon felt an uprush of affection and embraced Dana and pressed his cheek to Dana's cheek, and Dana kissed his cheek like a little boy who likes to be loved and is happy and loving.

Bob: "You've been having a look at Temple? How does it seem?"

Dana: "Well it looks all right. I haven't seen any money floatin' around." ("Floatin'"—he really means like autumn leaves on the stream.)

Bob had pointed out a stand of white birch half a mile up the hill. His property line (Dana's old place) was there. Dana said, "You see those spruce right over the car there? That's where the corner is." The spruce were at the lower end of the birches, not a large stand. It was surprising that he could see so well out of that little triangle of one eye.

"How've you folks been? Have you been gettin' along? Well that's good. It looks nice." ("We're trying to bring the fields back."—Rita)

"I'm doing poorly, but better than I was. I don't sleep so good nights, and there's pain in this knee I'm takin' some medicine for (foah). If I was younger I'd rather be out here. Do you know I woke up last night. I was dreamin', and in my dream I was tellin' them how old I was. (Laughs) Yes. In February 1979 I'll be 99. (Laughs) I'm 98 now." ("You've lived a long time, Dana. Not many people get to live that long.") "That's true. My son is doing poorly. He might not live as long as I" (and such is the Oedipus schmedipus complex, such is that universal rivalry, that Bob and Rita smiled, and Dana smiled).

He took us to the old creamery by the tracks in West Farmington, now a shell, falling apart. But the loading platform was still (mostly) standing. "There's the loadin' platform. We used to back the wagons right up to it. It was built in 1908. It belonged to the Turner Center creamery, then I think a company named Worrel took it over in 1918."

We drove on up the dead-end road above the creamery. "I think they made butter. They shipped the cream down to Turner on the railroad. Before the creamery was built we loaded it right into a box-car. Used all kind o' tricks in the wintertime to keep it from freezin'. I used to put blankets over the cans, and kerosene lamps under the blankets." The road ended in a large sandpit. Tracks, creamery, sandpit, all close to the river.

He asked me to stop on the road above Varnum Pond. "I thought we could look at the pond a while. This used to be all clear. There was a big pasture here, and a set o' buildings right up in there." Couldn't see past the alders and scrubby woods.

He had pointed out to me—on the Intervale Road—where his younger brother had lived. "He's dead now."

"My younger brother and I used to cut ice here for the ice houses."

The other side of Slim's store. "This is where they used to stack the squares for the mill. There was a sawmill here. The squares was two by two and four foot long."

"Did you ever haul for Voter?"

"No . . . just once. He had a load of milk in his car, just like this, and he skidded on the ice. It's a pretty steep hill. Well, they asked me if they could transfer it to my wagon. . . ."

"I made some money then, but it went."

The steep hill from Isalo's (Dick Blodgett's now) to Slim's store. "It was hard to get up in the winter if you had much of a load. For braking

I used to use two wheel chains comin' down. I had my own team (pair) and sometimes my dad loaned me his."

Recognized Ted. "Anybody livin' in your old place up there? Anybody livin' at Doctor Little's?" (His milk route used to go up the Day Mountain road, down past the Kennison's, down the long hill, over Temple Stream at Doc Little's. Then, "I used to go five miles beyond Docktuh Little's. I imagine if I was to take anybody up that way today, they wouldn't believe I could drive in so far.

"I used to set out at three in the afternoon, and my dad would meet me at three in the mornin'.

"There's the old pump house. Now the water line goes right down over in there. When we go back down (day-own) I'll show you where it comes out."

The milk route: "I had to start at three in the afternoon to get to the station at W. Farmington by five in the morning. I suppose I'd rather work in the day, but the money was good.

"I was born in Temple. The house was in Temple and the stable was in Weld. Do you know Wilder Hill? Well, you go up over the top, and then down, and you come to a flat place. Do you know Alder Brook? Well, it was down in there. But when I went to work haulin' milk, my dad had the place on Center Hill, and I lived there until . . . oh . . . I can't remember . . . oh, it's funny . . . what were we speaking of? Oh, yes . . . well, that house on the Intervale, that was when I got married. Nineteen-two it was. And I sold it in . . . ."

(Leon: "Sometimes he talks at night, he hallucinates, I guess. He'll call out: 'Now you watch the cows. I have to go away a while.' ")

Two of the old men at the nursing home are of the big, sour, arrogant, judging, patriarchal, independent type you occasionally see around here, unpleasant, repellant, yet impressive in their centeredness and competence. Another—a pipe smoker—has that judicious, reflective air of the independent thinker, and must also have been a farmer. Terrible to see them reduced to this. They are at a disadvantage they never would have accepted in their prime; the reduction is severe, and to some seems to be painful. Dana is twenty years older than any of them and has an extraordinary accepting spirit. Later, while I was trying to relax at the Fiddleheads Bar, I thought of his demeanor buttoning his inexpensive, much worn cardigan, or checking the little case to see if his glasses were in it, or asking me to open the drawer of the bedside stand and hand the little purse to him—this snap-purse, old, old, but the leather still holds, though one of the inside dividers (coins from bills) is gone—that demeanor that is so without egotism, unselfconscious, just doing the task and being entirely what he is, with his twisted fingers and odd little two-lump nose. I thought of his face and of the delusions of grandeur I've seen in so many writer friends, and of the overweening ambition, overweening conceit of so many academics and intellectuals. Had felt exactly this reading *The House of the Seven Gables.* Whatever strangeness there is in the depths of Hawthorne, that charming and generously given vitality of speech is so rare, so golden and musical, and so fascinated (perhaps loving) in its close, persistent attention to daily things; and then the critics (excepting James and Hawthorne's own friends, who knew what a gift he was), that whole menagerie of baying, deep-voiced, snapping, gnawing little creatures—how starched, bloodless, and anal all that self-conceited *understanding of it* appeared to be; and how grotesque to vie with the artist himself on the grounds that one understands his work perfectly! And I think of Norman crossing the streets of Madrid with one hand in the air to stop traffic for his imperial little self—and I know that what he is doing is mere triumph over the Norman that cowers, and maybe the drivers know this too; and I think of him sitting back cross-legged, imperially at ease, cigarette in the air, speaking the insight-that-resolves-the-argument in a quiet, quiet voice so that everyone says "What? What?" and leans forward, and unhurriedly and still leaning back, he repeats exactly what he has already said. He has become a figure, a special personage to a sycophantic circle, all the members of which have been repellant to me. And I think of Ted's *groupies,* and the figure that he has created and that created (demanded) *them,* though Ted is estimable in many ways. This streak in him is more delusion than ego, downright pathology, but as if sequestered; he's also wonderfully sane, modest, interested. . . What a remarkable character Dana has! What remarkable health! (For the truth is that Norman put these mannerisms—this *personage*—together in the process of recovering from paranoia and attempted suicide. It is not real arrogance, but imitated or feigned arrogance; *immediately* under it is despair.)

DICK BLODGETT

I went over to Dick's place to talk about some bookcases. Beautiful views on three sides, autumn hills and fields. In the shed/garage (attached) two large bird wings. "Oh, that's a goose, a Canadian goose. George shot it. Yes, and we lost it. Isn't that awful! It went bad. I had it soaking in baking soda, and I put ice cubes in, but it just wasn't cold enough down cellar. . . ."

Dick had a cold. "I shouldn't have gone out yesterday, but I've been trying to get some of the snowmobilers to swamp out some trails with me, and yesterday was when they could do it, so I thought I better show up."

He was drawing diagrams: packing crates for a complicated display booth he had built for a local businessman. Got out some vodka. Supper on stove. House terribly overheated, but everybody here is used to that. As always, talk of sports.

"Where've you been? Haven't seen you for a while. We called you a couple of times for poker. Did you get to see the fight (Ali-Spinks)? I was disappointed. He's about used up, I think. But the pre-lims were good, weren't they? Yes, I thought they were real good."

And soon: "The best ball game I ever saw in my life was the Braves and the Dodgers down in Boston. Warren Spahn was pitching. Oh, he was something else. And that great big colored man, what was his name, well darn it I almost had it! Catcher—right! Campanella, Roy Campanella. But I don't know, I think the players today are faster at everything, and they get paid so much. Oh, I think they are. Look at track. Don't you remember how long it took them to break the four-minute mile. Glen Cunningham—he was the big runner when I was in school. I was too small for football—I was just a peewee in high school, I got my growth later. But I was a good runner. I ran everything from the hundred to cross-country. Yeh. One of our local boys here, from Phillips, was the national champion in cross-country. Marty Toothaker. Yeah. I figured I was doing good if I could see him finish. When you see him today you'd never guess he was a runner. He can hardly get out of his own way (laughing) . . . a great big belly on him . . . But hockey was my game. I was a good skater and fast on the ice. I used to skate with the high school team when I was a freshman. I wasn't *on* the team, I just worked out with them . . . and then the next year they took hockey out completely, said it was too dangerous, or something. Oh, wasn't I disappointed!"

(I've heard about the local skating: because they used to cut ice from the ponds and the new ice was good for skating until the next snow. Now the snow piles up and no one skates.)

He let me have the bill for the last job. He's held it for six months—a peculiarity of his.

EDDIE

I took him the three dollars for gluing and sanding the little stool. Gave him a five. We were standing just inside the door of his little shop. (Every time Eddie glues a chair the legs are uneven—it's because the floor of his workshop is uneven.) He had already said, "Nice day, isn't it?"—sunny and brisk after three days of bitter cold and hard wind. (These are not banal remarks, but little prayers and attestations of an underlying joy.) The wide door to the little shed/shop was open, plenty of light. He was peering into his wallet. I could see that there were two ones there, together with a couple of fives and a twenty. Suddenly an outburst, angry, out of patience—"I can't see a goddamn thing!" He gave me the singles. I questioned him, since I knew it would have to be serious, even extremely serious, before Eddie would mention it. "Do you need new glasses?"

"They can't fit me for glasses anymore. They can't give me a tamn t'ing. I've got cataracts."

"Can't they take them off?"

"They're not ripe yet. It may take six months, it may take a year."

It was clear that the sudden dependency and inability to work was frightening, painful, and humiliating, since he's fiercely independent. "I've been putting the drops right to 'em. Damn them!"

"Can you drive all right? Do you feel safe driving?"

"No, I don't feel safe—I can't see that well any *more!* Especially on days like this. All that light from the snow. On a cloudy day I can see a little. It's all blurred. It's getting hard to see in here." (Hard to make the axe handles and the fiddles he's been making.)

"Nellie doesn't drive, does she?"

"No, she don't."

I asked what he'd do about shopping. "Well, there are people who say they'll take us in whenever we need it—but I hate that, it's goddamn monotonous. Nellie has to go to the hospital maybe three times a month—she's got the sugar diabetes. I have to go twice a month."

I said we'd help. The idea of shopping like this disturbed him terribly, the idea of being dependent and beholden.

"We usually keep a good stock on hand . . . except there are things we need now and then. Damn Nellie always buys the smallest amount she can of anything, and she won't get more till she uses the last drop of it, then all of a sudden she has to have it. That's bullshit. If I buy a large amount I catch hell . . . ."

Bitter mouth, bitter eyes, silence. One can see how important good sense has become to him—it carried his competence and independence through several heart attacks. He needs it to cope with illness, age, poverty, and now this hastening blindness—and it's being defeated by the silliness, giddiness, irresponsibility, lack of foresight of this fat little woman-child, who is spirited and seems to have a loving disposition, though perhaps not for him.

"All you're payin' for is the gottamn jar . . . and with the cost o' gas . . ." (When he speaks excitedly, his French-Canadian accent is stronger.)

I remember: Nellie's father, mean, killed himself, never had a friend, couldn't even stand himself.

A crisis is beginning now in Eddie's life.

EDDIE II

I took back the violin case Mabel had borrowed from him when she bought the fiddle. He was in his shop—that highly organized, ship-shape clutter of so many things, so many tools and made things, and things in-progress: axe and maul handles, fiddle. His snow-blower near the front. His TV and tape recorder that he plays the fiddle music on and accompanies; his Aladdin heater with the coffee pot on top to keep the air moist.

Things in Eddie's shop: shower in corner (faucets, flexible steel hose—a slab of concrete on the floor, with drain) used only in summer. "I use the pond water when I get my pump hooked up, same as in the house—pond water for the flush and the bath tub."

Neatly tied coils of garden hose on pegs.

Axes and axe handles, mauls and maul handles.

Table saw. Electric drill hooked up with sanding papers (he used it to file a burr off the handle of my pocket knife).

Snow-blower.

Come-Along and chains, on spikes up high.

Stacks (small) of cut out slabs that will become axe handles. The four-foot pieces of ash are in a pile out in front of the shed. He splits them with wedges.

His cane near the bench-bed he rests on.

Squirrel platform. "I used to feed the birds, but the squirrel took it all, so I decided to feed the squirrel."

He has cataracts, not yet bad enough to be operable. I asked him how his eyes were. I hadn't seen him for several months.

"No better and no worse. Not much worse. I'm right in the middle. Maybe a year from now I'll be really blind and they can operate. They did give me a license. Can't go but twenty-five miles from home. I can see the road all right, but if I come to a patch of shade I can't see what's in it till I get right on top of it. It makes driving dangerous as *hell*. If somebody was standing there I wouldn't see them. And there's so many cars the same color as the road. . . . Well it won't be long now a man like me can't afford to drive, puttin' the goddamn gasoline up to a dollar a gallon. They won't get it from me. I'll put the old wreck on blocks. No place to go anyway."

Eddie's voice has the double lilt of rural Maine and Canadian French, which contend against each other, the French wanting to stress the last syllable and the Maine to drawl it. He's so direct and engaged in everything he says—like Becky—and part of this is his inability to read or write (except in so rudimentary a way that he never much bothers).

"Did Mabel get a new case? Who's playing the fiddle? My understanding was the youngest girl was. It's the kind of thing you have to work at for a while, and it's no use trying if you don't really like it. I play mine every day. I have records I put on and I play along with 'em." (He used to go around and make tapes when he would hear of a record he didn't have.)

I thought I would invite him to go fishing this summer. I asked him if he still went.

"No, I can't walk in the woods on this leg. Can't sit in a boat either, it's too stiff, I can't bend, it hurts like hell in here. I went out with Joe Mattine a couple times. He had a deep boat. I put a plank across the sides to sit on. I put blocks at each end so it wouldn't slip. That left enough room for my leg. But the poor guy died, so I haven't gone fishing."

EDDIE III

Rain all last night and today, never very heavy but all waters are high and our road is flooded. I drove through this morning and took the car to Eddie's. We'll walk in and out and pick it up there. Nellie gracious on the phone. She resembles Eddie in this. "Oh, of course you can, George, there's lots o' room!"

Nellie's mother watching TV. Seemed low in spirit, where sometimes she's bubbly. I could hear her watery breathing several feet away.

Nellie's Pug dog, fat like Nellie. One of Esther Johnson's.

Talked with Eddie about the flood control measures we've heard mentioned, such as raising the road five feet. He said, "Then where's the water goin' to go? If it can't get across the road it'll back right up the intervale, it'll go as far as the church, and instead of two houses bein' flooded there'll be five or six. They have to leave a place for it to go. And they can't raise the Intervale Road without raisin' the Day Mountain Road, and that means building a new bridge. . . ."

Everyone is angry with the Fish and Game Department for refusing permission to dredge the stream at crucial points. Available money has been eaten up in fruitless surveys conducted by bureaucrats.

He said, "Oh there's lots o' pond ice, not even black yet. It looks like it up at the other end, that's just water on top o' the ice. When it's about ready to go, it's all glare ice, and it looks black from the water showin' through. Then one day the wind gets it and peels it right off. It'll pile it right up on the shore down here."

I asked him if he'd ever bounced on the ice in spring. As the ice melts there comes to be a large air space under it. I've heard of kids bouncing up and down on the ice, which becomes springy.

He said, "I've heard of it. Takes a damn fool to do it. Sometimes it don't pay to be brave. Stands to reason there'd be a big air space under the ice. It melts on the bottom faster 'n does on top. And when the water gets high, it pushes the ice up, then it runs out. But if you fell through . . . even if you was a good swimmer you might not find the hole again. And you'd cramp up in the cold water, and that'd be the end o' you."

I said I was going to take a look at the pond. If the ice would hold me it would be a good shortcut home.

"Oh it'll hold you. It may be rotten at the edges. Here, take this (reject axe handle), you can test the ice as you go. . . ."

(The axe handle, roughed out ash, sharp edges still, and water-logged. He had seen an error early on.)

As I started off, he called, "If any o' those fish poke their heads up, give 'em a good whack."

The ice was rotten at the edge and for several feet out. I walked home the long way.

When I dropped the axe handle on the pile of ash logs going back, I could hear recorded fiddle music in Eddie's little shop.

EDDIE IV

"Mother had a string of goiters like a necklace right around her neck, each one the size of an egg yolk." The whole family had goiters. She went to the hospital to have them removed, age 37, "healthier than I am today."

"She went on a Thursday. Sunday morning she was dead. If it'd happened today they could've saved her easy. She died of loss of blood."

He sees my picket pin (for the pony). "You could open champagne with that."

Eddie was eleven when his mother died. He had two younger sisters, one younger brother, two older brothers, a father. The older brothers worked as hired hands, father in the woods.

"That was when I started cooking and taking care of things. There was no one else to do it. My father was hard to get along with. Those were hard times. I left home when I was fourteen."

TED'S HOUSE

Used to be a stage stop. "They spaced them every eleven miles. Apparently, that was a good run for the horses. The next one's in Phillips—that's where this road used to go—and that's about eleven miles. If they had one in Farmington, at least on the far side of it, that would be eleven miles. . . ."

"Some of the exits on the Maine Turnpike are ten and eleven miles apart, or twice that. I wonder if they evolved from the stage stops?"

"Some towns did. They got a lot of business that way, and got established. I imagine the stop in Farmington had sleeping accomodations. Here they probably just had snacks and stuff for the horses. Maybe hard cider. This place was famous for its hard cider, but that was much later, when old Bert Mitchell owned it. There used to be a big barn here—on the stone foundations just uphill—two or three times the size of that little one out there. And there was a carriage house. It was still standing just before I bought the place.

"There was a commercial apple orchard here when Bert Mitchell owned the place. The apple growers lost the market to Canada after World War I. Most of these apples were shipped to England.

"There were a lot of the old varieties here—Wolf River, Black Oxford."

They sold the big old iron cookstove. It never worked very well and couldn't hold a fire more than two hours. Now there's a large sheet-metal room-heater ("tin stove") that can be piled full and will burn all night. They cook on an electric stove in the corner by the windows.

"We're in an awful cold spot. Earl Barker used to have the place. He used to say he burned fifteen cords a year and was still cold. I said I'd burn twenty and keep warm but it's nip and tuck."

The kitchen is a one-story ell. Floor sags; table sags.

The room is battered, the walls and ceiling deeply discolored by years of wood smoke. Yet the room is clean, neat, homey, and attractive. There's a window by the table and two by the sink and stove. A good sized squarish room, with a large pantry and another storage room with a freezer in back. No running water now (the pipe broke several years ago)—old-fashioned wash basin and pitcher on a stand to the left of the refrigerator.

House plants in hanging pots in the window—ivy, spider plant, wandering jew, a couple of flats of lettuce from Alison's parents' greenhouse. Pussy willow in a jar.

Large paper lantern over the central ceiling light. Large Mexican glass-and-tin star over the light above the table.

On the table: jar of chopsticks, plain, good-looking old fashioned tea pot, salt shaker, "loot" from old houses.

"How many things here did you gather from abandoned houses?"

"Practically everything! You name it! Pots, pans, dishes, silverware, egg beater. I don't think we've ever bought anything . . . oh, maybe a few bowls. And a few of the things—the good plates—belonged to my grandmother."

By the wood stove there's a woven basket (Indian—Earl Knockwood, actually; Mabel gave it to them) filled with firewood.

Bamboo chimes on the door—not attractive.

Silhouette portrait of Jake on the wall. Japanese colored print: "Japanese Audubon—Cid sent it to me. It's around 1880."

Poème concrete: "Heart Hearth"—clumsy, like much of the artwork and decorations.

Framed botanical print. "What is it?"

"Gelsemium."

"What's that?"

"Jasmine."

A handsome, small print.

Framed pressed spray of a heather-like twig. "That's Empetrum Nigrum. Black Cranberry. Empetrum means 'on a rock.' It's an arctic heath. I got this down around Bar Harbor. But you remember our famous outing on Saddleback? The rescue expedition? I saw some up at the top. You don't find it much south of here."

U.S. map on the wall, with some pins in it to show Ted's travels in the west—readings, residence teaching.

OUTSIDE, APPROACHING

The paved road ends in a fork of dirt roads—the left of which is not actually a road, but Ted's driveway, which is lined on the right by three big maples, and on the left, one. (It was under this one, a free-standing heavily leaved tree, that Ted and Alison were married by Peter Mills.)

Clam and mussel shells in great abundance, spread like paving at the top.

Slope rises gently to left of house: a small field; six or seven apple trees (many more in the higher fields and uphill in back of the house).

A beautiful site by the stream, old mill race rapids, a flat place, big trees. Used to be trout in this stretch but it has been heavily fished for years.

The house sits crosswise at the end of the drive (presently rutted and mucky), one gable end pointing down toward Temple Stream and the now unoccupied trailer where Elliott Hodgkins died a few years ago, the other gable end pointing uphill. The entranceway—in the side—divides the house in the middle, one room on each side, same on second story. Small attached shed on the uphill side; another (Ted's miniscule study, or rather writing room—now displaced by the shack up the hill) in the corner where the kitchen ell was added.

The house is tall-looking and long, though it is not a large house. Unpleasant lines, decrepit. Some broken clapboards, the paint is peeling—a paint job never finished years ago, so that most of the house is dark red, but a patch is off-white. Black asphalt shingles on the roof. Two chimneys can be seen, one of which is missing several courses of bricks. (The kitchen chimney cannot be seen from the front.)

Three steps of granite slabs, cemented ends. A small platform porch without roof or rails, rotted planks, catches the snow from the roof all winter long. Patched with odd pieces of plywood.

Clothesline runs from the door to the big, free-standing maple in front. Another runs from the door uphill at an angle to a large, forked post.

Large tansy to left of the steps. "Usually you find these at the kitchen doors—keep out the flies." Sprawling clump of roses to right.

At the right hand corner of the house downhill is a large stand of lilacs. These are right at the edge of the steep short side slope that goes down to the dirt road. The lilacs are badly overgrown, like all the lilacs I have seen here.

Along the downhill end of the house and just behind it: crab apple, apple, pine, wild cherry, and a mass of new scrubby stuff. In early summer the crabapple—which is large—is covered gorgeously with blooms.

The kitchen is a one-story attached ell, with its own chimney.

To the left of the entranceway is a 6 x 4 garden (this is the south side) for early things: lettuce and peas, mostly. The main garden—small but well-organized—is in the ell of the house and barn/shed, on the uphill side, up to the raspberry stalks in the old cellar hole, thirty steps from the house. There are bean poles in the garden, some slender white birch saplings in the cellar hole. Right across the farm road that goes uphill into the upper fields and woods there's a sprawling, unkempt compost pile.

There used to be a plague of woodchucks nestled among the stones of the cellar hole. They demolished the garden a number of times. Ted kept a shotgun *in place* at the upper window—and had several meals of lettuce-fattened woodchuck. Now Angus, the mongrel Border Collie, keeps them out.

There are apple trees again on the slopes above and beyond the barn.

Adjoining the kitchen at right angles—going uphill—is a low, decrepit shed, weathered board sides, asphalt shingle roof, wavering ridgepole. This leads to the barn, set at right angles to it. The barn sides are a beat and weathered patchwork of gray barn boards and curled gray wooden shingles. Metal roof.

Across from the barn, at the far edge of the farm road, a *low* stone wall, not really a wall—a linear, low pile of fieldstones—ends the orchard.

SHED

Decrepit. Jumbled. The floor sags, as does the ridgepole. Open side entrance—a bay rather than a door (this is customary). The woodpile (not much left)—neatly cut and stacked.

Items: snow pusher (like a skiff with handles, removes snow faster than a shovel); garden cart, metal sawhorse (the Johnny Grant model, that he got from Johnny, as did I); aluminum extension ladder on its side; raccoon pelt draped over a rafter, never cleaned, glistening fat still on it (this is one I shot in my cornfield, and the dogs quarrelled over, and Ted and I ate); splitting maul and wedges (mine—on loan).

The outhouse is at the far end, patched with oil cloth. Usual odor, as of sewage, not excrement.

Items: Bearpaw snowshoes (nylon cord); red gas can; bike; small toboggan, small sled, small red wagon, two adult bikes (one is Alison's, the smaller Jake's); two scythes (called *snaths)*, a large, metal-frame bucksaw; some pieces of a wooden bucksaw frame; several large door hinges; some boards on a rack against the wall; clutter . . . clutter; cat carrier; roll of tar paper; small yellow truck (plastic toy), ski poles, pots, sections of old stove pipe; more yellow toys: steam shovel, pay loader; piece of tarpaulin; old snowshoes, *good* design, gut; rubber horse-buckets used for clamming; clam rake; crowbar; spade, grill, egg basket (metal) also used for clams/mussels . . . more.

BARN

The small barn seems to be more or less abandoned, though some things are stored here. There's another woodpile, just a pile, not stacked; some bed springs, wheelbarrow, broken chairs, broken barrels, broken phonographs, an old high chair, some platform scales, pieces of rusty ceiling tin with embossed patterns.

Everywhere the same combination of neatness and decay; the on-going decision of *what* to cope with (since *everything* cannot be tended to) and what to abandon in favor of more important things: Ted's work, music, reading. It is a house of readers, one can see everywhere what has been sacrificed in order to protect these pursuits.

VINT AND FAMILY

Vint called to say he couldn't stand the dogs keeping him awake anymore, fighting and barking and even crawling under the house at night, would I come down and get them, it had been three days now.

The cause of all this was that one of their wrinkled, chubby little Pugs was in heat. There wasn't a chance in the world that she'd let either Shem or Woody mount her—those giants—yet they couldn't know this and couldn't shut down the terrific drag of that mechanism.

Pleasant to walk into that house (that is more like a camp; a trailer with an extra room, a wooden roof, a wooden entranceway). Rusty wasn't there, but the seven others were, plus Rhonda's boyfriend, plus Leonard Bardin, plus Vint and Sue.

Rhonda and her boy were kissing and embracing at one end of the sofa, lost in a sweet stupor of sexuality that everyone tried to ignore, was constantly aware of, and obviously enjoyed. They were watching the same program here that Becky and Michael were watching at home, Judy Garland in *The Wizard of Oz*. Karen, Stacy, Sue, Mark—all were crowded onto the same sofa that Rhonda and her boy were on.

Big, color TV. Two sets here, two antennas. Vint says, "The kids want to watch their programs and I want to watch mine"—except that he wasn't watching his, namely the Holmes-Ocario fight and Norton-Shavers. He put these on after theirs was over. Vint dominates enormously here and with his huge Sumo wrestler's body gives off a great aura of authority and masculine will. The kids say, "You gotta watch out for him at night—he gits ugly." But there's real sweetness and generosity in him, too. Some of the kids know how to get around him. When Kevin insisted on coming up to my place with Cecil and Leonard, Vint stormed out of the house and yelled at him ferociously, "Git back in here mister. You ain't goin'!" But Kevin, his face writhing with complaint-innocence-and-explanation said, "Woody's off in the woods. I gotta help. It takes three of us. He keeps runnin' off. You can't git near 'im," etc., etc., so reasonable and objective-sounding that one could see Vint cogitating upon it and being swayed from his wrath.

The marriage is an unusually happy one, not without storms. (Vint was facing indictment for rape several years ago, but the case was dropped. Eddie said, "He's been rapin' her every weekend for three years.") One of the charms of the place is that the people are all pursuing their creature comforts and enjoyments in such a naive, childlike way. The whole family hunts. There's a case (glass front) of rifles on the far wall. (Some are a neighbor's, kept here for safety against the predictable coming flood. Vint's floor might get wet, but the water reaches window level in the other house.) And there are fishing rods in the entranceway and in one of the sheds. Canoe out front in summer. Sometimes a snowmobile in winter. The yard out back is big enough to play softball, which one often sees the whole clan doing. There's a horseshoe pit as well, and an extremely pleasant swimming place in the stream that borders their property. They have a picnic table set up near it. There's no family around that enjoys life so well as this one. Karen is Susie's best friend and Susie is down there often. Shem goes to the swimming hole in the summer, accompanying the children. He stands in the water almost chest deep, nose close to it, peering down, peering, peering—then abruptly he plunges his head under water and forages with rigorous thrusts. He's fishing. He keeps it up year after year, though he has never caught a fish and never will.

Vint says, "They was under the floor last night. Used to be only Missy could get under there, but they broke out a lot o' boards and went under. I come pretty close to gettin' my shotgun last night." The boys laugh approvingly at this display of upcountry machismo—but when, a little later, Vint invites me to drink some coffee with him, and we sit alone in the kitchen, and I say to him seriously (since I'm disgusted with Woody), "Actually, shooting him might be the best thing. I don't know how the kids would take it, though"—he says immediately, "Oh, I wouldn't do that"—though it turns out that he has just shot two of his dogs. (Vint reminds me of Eddie in this respect: that is, he is genuinely kind to animals, develops real affection for some— Sashka, for instance—yet is brutally expeditious in wiping certain of them out.) He had killed the two large ones. I asked him why. "They was raisin' too much hell with the neighbors. They was after the rabbits next door. Not that they killed any. . . ."

"There was one frozen in the ice and they dug it up. . . ."

" . . . and John thought they killed it."

"He's pretty mad at Sashka, too. He told Mabel he'd shoot her—Mabel said go ahead."

Vint said that Hervey Andrews had just killed his black Labrador. The dog couldn't learn not to bite "hedgehogs" (and Vint adds, "porcupines"). Hervey was tired of paying the vet to pull quills.

Vint praises Sashka. "She's my honey. She sleeps right under my bed every night. And when I drive into town she comes right along beside me. The only thing about her is she's snappy around the kids."

"Yes," I say, "she's high tempered," and I tell how she'd treed the raccoon last year and lit into Shem when he tried to take it after I brought it down with my pistol. Shem had a crick in his neck for several weeks. He'd been astonished at her ferocity.

Kevin and Cecil kept trying to get a rope around Woody. Once they used the Pug as bait and almost succeeded—but Woody is terribly spooky, skittery, watchful, panicky. After several attempts to corner him he withdrew into the nearby woods.

Someone had the bright idea of taking the Pug in the car and driving up to my place; Woody would follow. Kevin and Cecil and Leonard came, Leonard holding the Pug. Kevin played the flashlight over a thicket at the end of the field—a pair of eyes glowed. "There he is! See 'im! See his eyes?!"

Cecil banged on the side of the car and barked. We drove slowly. Leonard said, "He'll git the scent all right. He'll come along. Won't he, Missy. Sure."

He did come. Shem was in the car with us and was no trouble. Neither had eaten for three days. Shem was exhausted.

At the house we took Missy inside and left all the doors open. At last Woody came in—and Cecil sprang to the door and closed it. I drove them home.

Late that night Mabel got up to go to the bathroom and saw that Woody wanted to go. She let him out—and watched him run off down the road while she stood there calling him.

Today we repeated that elaborate maneuver—and Woody is now

chained to the porch. It's raining, but he can take shelter in the dog house I made for him—in fact is in there now.

And Sashka, who was here briefly, is down at the Harrises', under Vint's bed.

HERVEY ANDREWS

"Well, I know what I used to do in spring. I used to pick up some beer and go down to Slim's camp and we'd fish for Togue . . . but he's gone now. . . ." When people say this of Slim they say it with unconscious feeling. He was not just a neighbor, or a presence in certain lives, but was important in many lives. He and Hervey were close, though Slim was twenty-five years older.

Hervey must be about thirty-five now. He's aging fast because he works so hard and suffers the usual boredom, though he doesn't have a minute left over in the week. It's the lack of *return,* lack of pleasure, lack of excitement that drags them all down—and Hervey *gives* far more than most, is a serious, considerate, responsible person, who feels resentment and feels that he is burdened. He works as a mechanic for the school district, but his character is like that of the old farmers. He has been Road Commissioner for several years, but now has given it up. "I just didn't have time. I was out evenin's an' weekends. After nine hours a day that's just too damn much."

He was passing our turn in his pickup truck and saw Mabel, Becky, and Michael wading through the flood water and drove them home. I came downstairs and had a drink with him and we talked.

I said, "You got through the flood okay."

"Oh yeah, if you don't go too fast you can make it—least in the truck I can."

"That's not a four wheel drive, is it?"

"No, but I can go just about anywhere I want."

I asked him about the project rumors—raising the road, etc.

"No, they won't raise the road. If they do, that would make them responsible for the houses between the road and the stream, and they ain't about to do that."

"What's going to be done then?"

"Not much. Clear out the dead trees along the bank. Ha, ha."

"I guess that'll help some, but not much. I was watching it today. There weren't any dead trees in it."

"No. . . ."

I offered him some cheese and bread. "No thanks, that's all I been doin' today, is drinkin' and munchin'. I could tell the damn lunkheads what to do with that stream! Anybody that's lived here all their life can tell them. We used to dig gravel in that stretch between Vint's and Rosie Blodgett's. You could walk under the bridge and there'd be a couple of feet over your head. Now you have to damn near stoop to get under it. And we got all the gravel we needed, 'stead o' payin' three dollars a yard for it. And there weren't no floods. Damned educated idiots! They say it'd be bad for the fish spawning if we dredged it. But they don't spawn in that section anyway, and my God there'd be miles o' stream we wouldn't have to dredge. There's not many native trout left there anyway. And they stock the stream anyway. I don't know. It's discouraging. Same thing with the Sandy River. Everett Vining used to dredge up gravel at the bend just above the bridge, and there was always more the next year. Now they haven't let him do it for several years and that whole bend's just a mess o' gravel and the river floods worse than ever. Everett says he wouldn't touch that gravel if they paid him now, he's so mad. I tell you what's goin' to happen here, it's going to get like it was thirty or forty years ago, people are going to do exactly what they want, they're just gettin' sick and tired and fed up with government. All the things we could do with money, they had to take fifteen thousand and make a survey with it, takin' their goddam photographs and drawin' pictures of it. All they had to do was talk with someone that knows it. You know what the trouble is? The stream used to be on the other side o' the road and it keeps wantin' to go back. The old timers can tell you about that. And the whole Intervale's nothin' but gravel. They had an awful time drillin' the well at George Blodgett's. And when they put the sewer system in at the Barden's, every time the backhoe scooped up a shovel full the sides would cave in, they was just gravel, hardly any dirt at all. The stream used to flow all the way across, fairly close to the hill, then it came back to this side before the old Hamlin place."

He said, "I joined the Sandy River Watershed Association—not as Road Commissioner, just private citizen—that's all it is, just concerned citizens. The idea is to get permission beforehand to dynamite ice jams and whatnot. I think they're makin' some headway . . . not much . . . I tried to get other people here to join, but nobody had the time . . . so I got sick and tired of it . . . what with one thing and another I was goin' to meetin's and working on roads and whatnot every night . . . so I give it up. . . ."

Mabel said, "Isn't there any way to get Augusta to listen to you about the dredging?"

He said, "If you can think of one, let me know."

"It's the same with the zoning now," he said. "There's more rules and regulations . . . If I want to build on my own property I'm going to build on it whatever I want and just the way I want. Okay, you have to take care o' the sewage so you don't pollute the streams—nobody argues with that—but what's all this about settin' back from the road and havin' so much space on all sides?"

I said, "Dick Blodgett says it makes a hardship for lots of people. Those who don't have any money can't afford to clear a large lot, and can't afford to keep it open. And old people can't shovel a driveway in winter."

"That's right."

The Blind Man

Visiting the huge, heavy-drinking blind man, 80, who had been a farmer.

He talks of his farms, his exploits, holds out the bottle. "Get a glass up there on the shelf. This won't kill yeh. Not what made me blind. No, the woods did that. Yeah . . . yellow birch tree did it. My own damn fault. I was drivin' a bulldozer without no cockpit bars and I was pushin' on a yellow birch, got it hung up sideways on the way down.

Should've stopped right there and cut it loose, but I kept pushin'. Oh it whipped across my face. I'm lucky to be alive. But I'll tell yeh somethin', it gets to be a goddam bore sometimes. Ayeh. I've heard an awful lot of goddam radio. Well, say somethin', lemme hear yuh voice. Where you come from? What brought you here? How'd you light on this God-forsaken little town? What kind of a man are you? How tall are you? Do you mind if I feel your face? Push it over here. It's amazin' how much I can tell with my hands. And it's just as amazin' how little I can tell. See . . . I can tell you're losin' your hair, but I can't tell what color it is, can't tell how old you are, though there's a feel to the skin around about fifty that tells a lot . . . and you got that feel, yeh. You got a short nose but it juts right out, that's supposed to be a sign o' temper. You got a bad temper? Heh? You hell on the wife and kids, are yeh? You got a long upper lip. 'Course that's English and Irish. Lot of English here, most everybody 'cept the Finns and the Frenchies. Some Irish, too, not much. You good lookin'? You could be—got nice lines from the forehead over the cheekbones and chin, but that could be spoiled by all kinds o' things I can't tell by touch. You drinkin' that stuff I gave you or just sloshin' it around in the glass? Don't you waste it on me. Tell you what . . . you keep me likkered up and I'll tell you all the yarns you want to hear about the old days in Temple. Ayeh. Pure bullshit, too . . . best kind. Wouldn't you say so? Best stories are all ninety percent lies, sometimes a hundred. Too bad Vic Sawyer's dead. What a story teller he was! Some of it was true, too. Did you know there was a whorehouse in this town? Famous one, yeah—woodcutters used to come from miles around. Oh, t'was worth your life Saddy night! What a hullabaloo there was! You sittin' up straight? Your ears perkin' up? Ha ha! It's all shit, pure shit. Never was such a thing in this town, though God knows enough of us wished there was. This was a town of churches and Grange halls and little schools. Ayeh. No whorehouses, no whorehouses. Always had a few whores. Actually, they didn't take money, not straight out, and they wasn't much to look at, neither. God help us. How'd we ever pull through? Maybe we haven't.

[JOURNAL]

APRIL 1

The winter began early—frozen ground before the snow (which is bad for wells—rainwater can't get to them—and is bad in the spring run-off, because the ground can't absorb the melting snow and so everything goes into the streams, and they flood), and there were long spells, three to four weeks at a time, during which the temperature never got much above zero. But it was a good winter for skiing—no rain or ice (little thawing and re-freezing) and I had six or seven good cross-country outings, the best being over the old Avon Road (continues the Day Mountain Road) with the Kimbers and others. Susie came once. I had been afraid it would tire her, but she came in fresh and lively where most of us were tired. This old farm road gives you an inkling of what it must have been like in the days before motors. Orchards, grape vines (on old stone walls)—pear, apple, crab apple—fields, wood lots, here and there a cellar hole, huge trees by the road, not killed by salt. But the orchards are mostly dead or dying etc.

Spring began early. It was warming up seriously by the first week in March. Bob Leso, the forest ranger, came with his assistant March 9. I went out with them on snowshoes, toured part of the woodlot. Both young, pleased with their work, self-justifying work. At the end of the trek (four hours) Leso put on a burst of speed, left us far behind, covering a section by himself—it was a way of saying, "You see what I can do? You see how considerate I've been?" and to his assistant, "You see what experience can do?"

A week later we all went out again, Mabel with us this time, and toured another section of the 500-plus acres. Still good snow, but getting heavy. A week later (by then I was with dad in Florida) the snow was too rotten even for snowshoes, so the remaining tours have been deferred.

Ten days in Miami visiting dad at the hospital. Everyone had feared he was dying, but he rallied. And our loving sympathy somewhat abated as he got his strength back, since one must defend oneself against him—a tough old buffalo. Yet he and I get on well these days—I suppose since the time we spent together with mother. (He referred to it—"I could never have made it without you"—and wanted me to stay longer. We have more in common than either with any of the others.)

Flew back to Boston (straight from Jai Alai—losses; looked terribly fixed that night. My only wins were number hunches—a *quinella,* as the previous night a *perfecta).* Stayed with Ruth and Curtis, Chinese food, talk with Alan Berger. Drove to Portland in warm, deep-spring weather. And Portland was warm, though a couple of weeks behind Boston. Two days there, working, catching my breath. Then to Temple, April 1, in the evening. Here it is early spring, bare ground in the fields, but patches of snow too, and much snow in the woods and hollows and the north-facing hills. Still some flooding on our road, and a couple of huge holes. We had to leave my Saab and transfer things to the four-wheel drive Toyota.

Presents for everyone, lively scene and pleasant for me.

They were cut off six days by the flooding while I was away.

Temple Stream floods almost every year, often during the winter thaws (and then the flooded road freezes and is hellish for the rest of the winter) but almost always in spring. It drains a system of hills with more run-off than it can handle. The stream bed is piled with boulders and full of sharp twists at several places. Ice jams here, and uprooted trees, form dams. And then there are beaver dams that clog the flow and cause trouble. These I haven't seen, have been told of. I can't imagine how they lie; they don't block the stream itself; must be across some of the little arms and pools between here and the village.

Our road gets it from both sides: on one the stream, which parallels the road for a stretch and is never very far below road level; and on the other the pond and the outlet from the pond.

Beaver work has been extensive in the pond for the last few years. The level of the pond has gone up eighteen inches. The dam across the outlet has been dynamited several times, but the beavers restore it quickly. Often at night in the summer I've seen the glint of moonlight on the back of a beaver swimming in the outlet. This probably means the traffic is fairly heavy there. They dig under the bank so that the stream becomes a little wider but is hidden at the edge by the over-hanging bank, and they swim under the overhang. I've seen them too in the pond in the afternoon in summer.

The level of the pond is so high now that an arm of it has come right up to the road. Even a moderate rain will bring it creeping onto the road. And so for the first time in years the pond was opened to trappers. Tammy's husband, Steve, who lives by trapping now, took out thirty-four, many quite large. (I remember the first time I saw him in the woods, years ago—he was wearing his snowshoes upside down, so that the curved part bit the snow. These were shoes from the same man who outfitted Byrd to North Pole.) Another trapper took out five or six.

Our lower road was apparently under four to six feet of water (the stretch that lies between the pond and the stream). When this happens, the outlet reverses and carries water from the stream into the pond.

After the flood has receded the mud is sometimes too soft and deep even for the four-wheel drive. Long ago this was a corduroy road. Some of the logs still lie across it about a foot down. When the car wheels sink that low, you hit them with a thump.

APRIL 2

The whole area, the houses, roads, fields, woods—everything looks bleak and mangled, as it always does this time of year—punched, scraped, flattened, torn apart, bleached . . . and then mud-covered and in danger of being washed away. Only the streams are thriving, roaring day and night, at their mightiest. The fields behind the houses near the stream—from the old red schoolhouse to the church—are sopping wet and muddy from having recently been under water. Yet this staggering, hung-over condition only lasts a couple of weeks, and green spring pushes through.

The road to my cabin still has a foot of snow on it, though there are many bare places a few feet away in the woods. The tree trunks—dark, for the most part—attract heat and radiate it. The snow melts first around the bases of the trunks, and then melts between the trees, while the nearby road—even the parts that weren't travelled by snowmobiles—still lies under snow. The longest lasting snow is, of course, the compacted "boilerplate" of the snowmobile tracks. This is why they are damaging the fields and gardens: the soil stays frozen underneath them and can't be worked up for planting as soon as the rest. Late in the summer you can still see the snowmobile paths across the fields where the grass is stunted.

These patches of soiled snow on the dead sandy-brown meadow grass, with reddish-brown spikes of meadow-sweet, dark brown weed stalks and little sprouts two feet high that will be saplings—all this with the myriad trunks of trees behind it, almost black if they're wet. There's something in these colors and textures that excites me—days in early spring when I'd tramp around the woods and fields at home, in the outlying suburbs of Pittsburgh, or look at the long hill, the woods, and fields out the windows of the grade school (Kelton). These colors and scratchy textures are handled with great genius by Bruegel, who must have loved them. They are certainly northern. I've seen similar colors in portrait sketches—mixed media (and apparently there aren't many of these) by Holbein. Perhaps coincidence, except that I've never seen these combinations in Italian paintings. The combinations I mean are: soiled snow, tree trunks, dried grass.

The woods this time of year have the simplicity and luridness of certain Expressionist painting—Munch, especially, and our own freebooter, Ryder. The snow lies in great "organic" patches—undulating edges, curved and sinuous (these patches may be bounded, more or less and here and there, e.g. in low places, by contour lines). They are very stark against the murky black or dark-brown forest floor (leaves, muck) just freed of its snow and very wet. And then the tree trunks, especially if wet, are stark against the snow, branches still stark against the sky. Some of the skies now retain a wintry cast, but by and large are brightening as the sun brightens, are often quite blue and cheerful.

It rained heavily at night. Susie was staying at the Harrises', whose little trailer house was flooded (eight inches) last week. I began to worry—foolishly actually—about the stream flooding, thinking of the nightmare horror in my sister's life, when they were evacuated by rowboat from their home in West Virginia after flash floods had put the whole valley under water. She was carrying her infant daughter in her arms. The boat tipped and she fell into the water. Her husband jumped in to save the baby, but was struck by floating ice and almost drowned. The baby's body never was found. I walked down to the house. It was three in the morning. The rain had been fairly heavy for several hours. Poor Mabel had to wake up and tell me not to worry—it had taken several days of rain to lift the stream over its banks, all the way to the Harrises' house. And there had been heavy run-off from the snow.

APRIL 3

There are fat buds on all the trees (they began as little swellings in the depths of the winter), and the poplars, some of them, already have tiny leaves.

Ferocious wind today. The dogs were afraid to go out. Full moon. Power failure—trees down across lines. Read "Tin-Tin" to the kids by kerosene lamp. Sweet for me to feel this closeness again, after being away for almost three weeks.

APRIL 4

Power on. A calm day. The wind helped dry the ground—which is still wet, however. Yard around the house pocked by the ponies' hooves.

The snow is off the garden. The cat sits in the garden motionlessly. And Sashka digs for mice in the snowbanks downhill—listens, digs, listens, digs. The ponies wander in the wet field that was seeded last year.

We'll test our parsnips today or tomorrow.

Mabel has started tomatoes, okra, peppers, etc. on shelves in the windows.

On the poplars and red maples, the buds are almost leaves; same for the elms. There are great huge catkins on the basswood. The white birches seem ready to open, the buds are long. The sugar maples are not so far along yet.

Saw first robin on the way to the cabin. The dogs' prints in the oozy mud are splayed and large, as in the snow. One would think the dogs were huge.

The forest floor dried out a good bit by the day of fierce wind— shades of light brown, with here and there a rotten stump, and moss, a dim green, and gray rocks. The darkest shape is the wide, sinuous, temporary stream that carries run-off along the road, then under it and downhill to the swale where it becomes quite wide and swampy. There are tree limbs strewn across the road—such a pruning these winds give the woods—and the usual torn flags of birch bark.

The huge old sugar maple on the road by the tumbling house, just where the road turns to my cabin—this tree that looks so dead in the winter and does in fact have many peeled dead limbs—has sent out a great crown of buds, like the great oak that Prince Andrew sees in *War and Peace*.

APRIL 5

Rain last night, corn snow today, almost hail, soft hail. About an inch. Gray and wintry, but not cold. The twigs with their new buds, and the needles on the pine trees, are all sheathed in ice.

APRIL 6

Susie has been going to the public school for several weeks now, by choice. But there's a terrible waste of hours every day—three hours— just getting there and back. The children were not consulted when this centralization took place. She gets up at 5:30 or 6:00, reads in bed a while, leaves the house at 7:30, walks a mile down our muddy dirt road, gets on the school bus, and arrives at school shortly before 9:00. A generation ago that first mile of walking would have brought her to the little red school house.

A blue sky today with lots of white clouds, sun shining low in the east—and the ice-sheathed twigs of the trees are sparkling unbelievably.

I helped Susie with her homework last night. There were some mimeographed sheets written by her school teacher, or principal, or someone, little squibs about Maine and famous people of Maine— abominably written, dead, journalistic cliches with here and there mistakes of grammar. And then the usual phony question: *Which of these stories did you like best?* I hadn't criticized the stories—I don't want to queer things for her, and she hears good writing here at home— but she said, "I didn't like any of them." She'll make a mark by the least lumpy, and that will do. This awakened some long-gone memories of *coping with the culture.* We live so out of it now! All the dodges and tricky accommodations of city life, and my early youth.

APRIL 8

First sight in the morning: snow in the air, and three inches of snow everywhere—piled on the railings of the little bedroom balcony, and on the dilapidated picnic table out back, and on the cars.

Snow all day, coming down straight and slow, the large soft flakes of spring. They stick to the pine needles and pile up on the limbs of trees, and stick to the cabin roof and the house roof. The skylight at the cabin usually sheds the snow right away because it's so steep, but this snow clings to it, and is spread over it evenly—and the light inside is subdued, with an almost amber richness.

In early afternoon the quiet is disturbed by gentle puffs of wind. These are not strong enough to sweep the snow from the roof tops or the limbs of the hardwoods, but they agitate the springy boughs of the pines all around the cabin, and I hear a soft thumping everywhere as falling gobs of snow strike the snow on the ground.

Within an hour the wind has increased enormously. The pines are shrouded in a haze of snow as the wind stirs up all the snow left on them. This snow and the falling snowflakes are driven sharply in the wind coming from the west. Abruptly the quantity, the density of flying snowflakes, triples and everything is obscured in this flickering, agitated streaming whiteness. The wind has shifted and is blowing now from the SSW. The snowflakes are flying in long horizontal lines, broken by the complicated wind patterns of this little field in the woods that is part hillside and part level. Here and there in the swift horizontal flow there are columns of swirling snowflakes, and there are even pockets of stillness in which the big flakes are falling slowly straight down.

Twenty minutes later the quantity of snowflakes diminishes, but the wind is even stronger, and the flakes are streaming long long distances flat out, and the pine boughs that catch the wind are lifted and bent like bows and the clusters of needles bounce and stream in the wind.

An hour later the wind is still high, but there is no snow in it now. The sky is brighter, though it is still overcast and cloudy. The pines are dark green now, no snow left, but the hardwoods are all outlined in white. The wet snow survived the wind; it seems, actually, that the wind compressed it, glued it tighter to the trees.

The fields that yesterday had been bare brown grass are now white, five inches deep in wet snow. All the stalky weeds—the meadowsweet and Queen Anne's lace—that had been covered by the deep snow of the winter show starkly against this background of new white.

There is an alternate brightening and darkening as the sun finds openings and then is covered again. Forty-five minutes later the wind is coming in powerful gusts, the clouds have been pulled apart, there are great patches of blue sky, and the sun is bright.

At night the wind is still strong, perhaps even stronger. The dogs don't want to go out.

Sights of the storm: out the kitchen window we see the black Shetland pony standing patiently in the streaming flakes and the downpouring flakes. She stands motionless, her head drooping and one hind foot slightly cocked. The long black strands of her mane, fringe—a spectacle of dumb endurance, some calamity of the old west, though she isn't suffering at all. The snow blankets her rear and back, almost an inch of it.

I remember the granular snow, or rather ice pellets, that covered the ground several days ago to the depth of an inch—and the peculiar sound of walking in it. Each stride kicked up pellets ahead and they scattered audibly, like spilled bird shot, especially when I was going downhill and they rolled noisily for two or three feet. All that melted the following day, and it seemed that spring was coming right on. But this now is a reversion to winter.

Tommy and his girl friend are here (their VW is stuck on the road). Both are living in the Yale Psychiatric Institute halfway house. I talked for several hours with Tom at breakfast. My own schizy make-up gives me great access to his experience; we share certain problems and certain joys, perhaps in different degrees. The schizy child-presence is there, and it's this that I find sympathetic and can talk with.

APRIL 9

Bright, windy. Last night the temperature was no better than fifteen degrees, but now (afternoon) the snow is melting.

I stayed up late baking bread (eight loaves) by the laborious method I hit on and that gives such good results—building up the loaves of rolled-out layers, almost as thin as pie crust, and painting each layer with water.

Tomorrow is Easter and Mabel's birthday. Tommy and his girl will leave after breakfast, which we'll make do as a birthday breakfast, if I can figure a way to cook the turkey in time. The kids are downstairs with Tommy and the girl. Mabel is at a meeting devoted to the upcoming anti-nuclear-power demonstration in New Hampshire.

When Susie and I last went to town we bought a couple of potted plants for Mabel's birthday. And I have a canvas shoulder bag for her.

APRIL 10—EASTER

Mabel's birthday. The kids were up at 5:30, and came in to get me, came clambering on the bed, looking all lit-up and wonderful. Michael strides back and forth in the bed, right on me and over me. One effect of the great patience Mabel raises them with—the combination they've had of great liberty plus lots of attention, lots of mothering—is that their excitement never makes them clumsy, is never more than they can handle, but looks wonderful. This comes from the harmonious development of mind/hand, hand/eye, appetite/desire, etc. etc—which isn't possible if they aren't free to experiment and make mistakes. (Play with food, break cups, etc.—which I probably couldn't endure if I were alone with them.)

Mabel and I had stayed up late the night before fixing the Easter baskets and hiding jelly beans. The baskets were placed by the kids' heads as they slept. (I tied Susie's to the hanging plants by her bed in her richly cluttered—an orderly clutter, actually—corner by the dormer.) They had already found the baskets, were waking me to watch the jelly bean hunt. I had placed a lot of easy ones for Michael and mentioned it to the girls, who were wonderful about helping him. They do this kind of thing without greediness or harsh competitiveness. For the difficult hiding places we did "hot/cold."

Pleasant breakfast while Tom and his girlfriend Ruth slept. The turkey was in the oven and Mabel was baking a cake. I had done the cooking for the past three days or so, now she was baking her own birthday cake.

Tommy like an exposed nerve, but much improved. His girlfriend more disturbed than he. He seems to be taking care of her.

APRIL 11

A little butterfly, about the size of a guitar pick (and if the pick were of horn, the same color) beating this way and that over the patches of snow near the cabin.

Gorgeous blue sky. Mild.

APRIL 12

Beautiful spring day. I came down from the cabin early—preparation to leave for Vermont. Mabel greeted me brusquely: "Nell just called. Your father died last night. She wants you to call Adele."

This was not unexpected. Nell had called several days ago to tell me that his heart was fibrillating, he was getting oxygen, the doctor had told her to notify the family. I called Adele. Dick called from Minneapolis, not knowing that Nell had already told me. He said, "I hope I go as easily. He had everything taken care of, right down to the last detail. Of course it helps to know where you're going"—a strange tone, part conceited, part didactic—and pious. "Well, I'm conducting a successful career . . . etc."

I told the children. It rolled off Becky, who is too young to let such things register. Susie looked shocked and dismayed. "He died?" That reaction touched something in me; I went out of the room crying.

APRIL 23

Rain last night, overcast today with occasional blue and sun breaking through.

The peepers in the swampy flats have begun their night-time chirping that sounds like masses of crickets—not yet the incredible, pulsating screaming of May, but getting louder.

There is still ice in some of the ponds, and clumps of snow in the woods. The road to the cabin is wet, running still and still spongy with the oozy, utterly bodiless mud of thaw. Wherever one goes in these hilly woods this time of year, one hears the sound of running water. The pulsing sound that in a large stream can sound like a babble of voices, and that in a small one can sound (though muted) like a tree full of little birds at evening.

Upset and sad because of the failure of our family life—which for me means the failure of life here—I walked through the woods to Porter Hill, stopping at the cabin to drop off some books. I could hear a partridge drumming in the woods—hard to tell how far away, the sound is so hollow and so carrying. It begins with stately, emphatic, slow *thumps*—as if calling for attention and making a great display of *presence;* and then very rapidly the thumping accelerates to a flutter that loses loudness as it gains speed.

The newly-seeded (last year) southerly field has a lot of fresh green in it; and there was a haze of green in all the fields along the Sandy River between here and New Sharon (I took Mabel's Aunt Frances to the airport yesterday), and a pervasive, pungent odor—both sharp and musky—of newly-spread manure. The early fields have all been plowed.

Flickers, nut hatches, starlings, swifts. I saw a partridge in a tree at the edge of the Porter Hill fields.

Sashka ran up out of god-knows-where and joined me in my walk.

Elms and basswoods, and the poplars on the high fields are all in leaf—a bright chartreuse. The brown fields on Porter Hill are covered by this lovely spring green in the tops of the poplars, very bright against milk-blue sky. Long catkins on white birches; and some of the birches (not yet in leaf) seem to have sprouted new twigs, look feathery against the sky—drawn in black lines.

Sashka hears a noise in the woods and dashes off. The woods are alluring this time of year—full of animal activity.

The old house at the end of the cabin field crumbles more every year, sagging in on itself, filling its rooms with fallen roof, fallen walls. Sky through the windows and half of the roof, sky and trees through the piecemeal walls. What's left of the roof has a sweeping of moss over it, and the moss has the same delicate bright green I see everywhere.

A huge wasp or bumble bee, gigantic and noisy, comes hurtling by as I walk. It follows me into the woods, but soon goes its own way.

The woods are a mess—strewn with fallen trees, fallen limbs, great tatters of white birch bark, debris of winter and the windstorms of spring.

The dead leaves on the little beeches—bleached looking, translucent, pale sand color, three and four inches long—look like little fish skewered through the gills and arranged in rows to dry in the sun.

I heard Sashka barking in the woods after we got back to the cabin. Ten minutes later she came in the open door with porcupine quills in her snout. There weren't many. I pulled them out with pliers. There was one in her mouth that was hard to get, and one broken one at the point of her nose that was harder still, as she kept flinching, dodging, squirming. It took twenty minutes to get those two. Later I discovered a broken quill in the side of her paw. I watched her eat, to see if she favored any part of her mouth.

APRIL 25

Three days of rain, that changed to snow last night and left a thin snow cover over everything—but then more rain melted it off. Now the rain has stopped, but it's cold, gray, and listless, like November, except that the brooks are roaring and there's a bright green haze over many of the trees.

APRIL 26

Warmer. Heard a loon down on the pond. The starlings are back, and some of the big roadside trees are filled with rooks, several hundred in a single tree, black and glossy along the branches, very decorative and sprightly.

Farmers tilling the big fields by the Sandy River, odor of manure—a dense, pungent odor with piercing elements (ammonia, probably) so that it combines the broad, pungent quality of tobacco with the sharp quality of vinegar. The odor is so strong and carries so far that one hesitates to say that it's pleasant—but it is not unpleasant. It is one of the country odors that one respects, perhaps is fond of without knowing it. It's an odor that is deeply reassuring, like the odors of sex and of good food. One inhales it and knows that life is right.

MAY 2

The trout stream—from Day Mountain Road down to Ted's mountain house (and I couldn't continue on down to Temple Stream as it was too dark to keep clambering over boulders, and I couldn't see to bait the hook). I walked home from there—seven hours all told, and exhausted.

The stream: at first alders and scrub growth, patches of blackberry canes, some slash. This entire area heavily cut maybe ten years ago. Many places hard to push through. Where the stream bed became deeper, the debris of the winter and of the spring floods was striking: bleached wood scattered this way and that, matted bark, grass, leaves lying in tangles here and there like gobs of hair—this establishes the high water mark. Also, on tree trunks near the stream bright orange wounds in the trees where ice barked them.

Then to a stretch where the stream bed was sandy and the banks level (this nearer the first big beaver dam). Then the large, almost circular basin of debris and muck, thousands of small sticks—say seven feet by two inches—a clutter, a basin of muck, and the remnants of the semi-circular dam broken by ice. A mile or so downstream they had built another. (But no fish in either, and none between them—maybe too new.) Then handsome stretches of stream, big trees. Caught three trout and spitted them on a small fire on a rock over the stream.

MAY 14

After the gathering at Nancy and David's (Jack's talk of Seabrook interesting—but the gathering dull, dull in a way I detest—them holding hands sitting in circle on floor singing and swaying), I dreamt that night of a marvelous party, crowded and with Scots and Britishers present, and maybe Irishers—all these, I think, because they're great talkers, and this co-counselling mob seems to hate talk. And my dream party was lively, inspired, dancing, talking, cavorting. Marty Washburn was there, elated, comic. A small Scots lad, very handsome, laid eyes on a diminutive Scots lass, very pretty and feisty, and they fell madly in love and she shouted a gay announcement of their troth: "Look what Fate has sent me! What a fine lad to wrap my shawl around! Which I will! I'm his forever, and may he use me heavily and reductively."

That phrase *heavily and reductively* delighted me in the dream. Later I wondered where it had come from.

MAY 16

Fished again in the evening, lower stretch of the brook that passes Ted's mountain place.

The stream—and to some extent its banks—is organized by the fact that water flows in one direction. Dead wood is oriented downstream, parallel to banks or at shallow angles, pulled that way by flood and ice. Tremendous amount of dead wood—sticks, logs, trees—some of it comes from slash and is pulled down by flood until it catches on banks. Where banks are steep it's surprising how far up the ice marks are. Other on-going factors: the continual crumbling of the banks, exposure of tree roots, death of trees, which then fall into the stream and are re-arranged by ice and current. All this dead wood, barked by ice, is bleached gray, or sandy, or almost white. The stream bed is so rocky it would be astonishing if one were not used to it. Boulders, stones, rocks. One can often go a great distance by hopping from rock to rock. The feel of this, balancing, and the water rushing away underneath, shallow, a foot or so, with pools of up to five or six feet deep. Boulders predominantly gray. Small leaves on the trees, pretty against sky. Hemlock, yellow birch, red maple. At two places there are deadwood dams, fair sized trees (yellow birch) that fell, got wedged and collected debris. Good trout pools just below these dams.

Hellebore, witch hazel in blossom, trillium in blossom, and by Temple Stream, the edge of Rosie Blodgett's field where I gathered fiddleheads, there were violets. Wild strawberry blossoms.

Spring comes in a rush when it finally decides to come. So much happens at once that you can't keep track of it—it's like being tumbled by the surf or a fast river. Fiddleheads grow in the flood margin of the big streams, wooded but not dark—sandy, leafy, twiggy soil. The swallows and the daffodils both appeared around the 10th of May.

MAY 19

The apple trees are in full blossom. Day breaks at around 5:00, and the morning is loud with bird song. The woodpeckers are like a percussion section. One raps at the eave of the barn (and that huge structure is his sounding box, or drum), and another answers from the woods, rapping on something more resonant than a tree—I don't know what.

A lot of tent caterpillars this year—I hope not the invasion of the gypsy moths that wasted Connecticut and Long Island. The school kids could wipe them out with a few concerted campaigns, but this is not a likely event in the school bureaucracy.

MAY 21

Starlings building a nest in the eaves of the house, swallows busy in the barn. Robins have already laid their eggs.

MAY 22

A late, cold spring, but the grass out back is eight to nine inches high now, and the gusts of wind speed across it in waves, agitations, tossings, more nervous and electric than water agitated by wind. And since, on this hill, the wind whirls and comes from several directions, we see this tossing as sometimes a dark green (when the top edges are bent toward us) and sometimes flashes of a silvery green as the wind shifts and reverses the bending of the grass so that the silvery undersides are seen.

Picking fiddleheads on the muddy flood-strewn banks of Temple Stream, with Becky and Michael. Going down by canoe (water still quite high), a delightful little trip, just right for the kids—small dangers (overhanging boughs, tiny rapids—they had to duck their heads and pull in their hands). Becky loved it, Michael was dazzled.

In the evening the barn swallows fly around the house, just as the ponies take their evening gallop round and round. But the swallows are so fast!—they *hurtle* through the air in remarkable dips and swerves—a dozen birds now, several generations, probably. I love them. They're beautiful and swift, like trout and dolphins. One sees the pride of life, and the joy of life in them.

MAY 29

Driving through the valley, the intervale, mid-afternoon, after a rain. Mist is rising—the green fields by Rosie Blodgett's, the trees at the edges, first the smaller ones (those that are invading the field, and then, close in back, their towering parents)—many shades of green, with frequent black limbs and trunks of *dead* trees, and slender living trunks still dark from the rain—all seem behind a veil of mist and in their many shades of green, with the dark shadows of their depths—dark now, where in winter the light of the snow makes the woods penetrable.

MAY 31

Total explosion of leaves, bushes, bracken, grass—all spaces are smaller. *Deep* blue skies, big dark and light clouds.

Bobby Thorndike building a fence for us—Bruce, Brian, Barry helping him. They work wonderfully well together, Bobby a perfect big brother, much affection and easy subordination among them. A pleasure to hear Bobby encouraging, praising, chatting, and giving orders in an easy-going serious way. I thought there's real love between the parents.

JUNE 28

Writing clears my head of emotion, it attaches obsessive emotion to thought, which is my only hope of purging myself of the unassimilated past. This is probably what I mean by "meaning." This mingling of emotion and thoughts. It's my way through to freedom. When I achieve it I feel the joy of liberation—or rather, simply, I feel joy, am light, illuminated, an energy field, a clear sky of energy.

The fishing trip with Dick, George, Charlie, Jules—two generations, all working men. I'm more than ever aware of my alienation from them—my privileges, education, rewards—the whole of my experience. Their virtues impress me. They are all modest men, but they have great pride (tempered by their conventions of dependence—on job, government, etc.—though otherwise they are independent men). Their modest endurance, their unhappiness, their relative contentment. All were born here, and are much attached to the way of life—hunting, fishing (at which all are expert), snowmobiling, poker, TV. Their relations with each other are entirely without revelation of self—lack even moments of simple expressiveness—yet they seem actually to be held together by feelings of love and they care deeply for one another.

We fished on the land owned by another local family, also of long establishment here—the Moshers—who had gone to school with Dick and Jules (they share childhood memories of fishing trips, etc.) but have been lumbering their own 10,000 acre tract, worth maybe three million. The lumbering road that winds up their massive hill was barred by a huge locked gate, but Jules and Dick have always had keys to it. We drove to a swampy meadow just over the top—a drowned meadow, actually, a quiet large pond ten to twenty acres created by beavers. Dead softwoods stick up here and there as gray and straight and barren as telephone poles—except for stumpy, sharp branches usually near the top. Meadowsweet also juts above the water. I fished from the beaver dam, Dick and Jules from atop the beaver house, George and Charlie from the canoe. A huge beaver swam in S-curves from somewhere near the edge to the dam, which he crawled over quite close to me, big as a large dog.

Fog, red-winged blackbirds gracefully planing from tree to tree, slow and impressive, as there wasn't any wind at all, cedars, mountain ash (Dick had transplanted some to his yard)—quiet, an extraordinary calm. The trout here are native, not stocked. The meat is as red, almost, as salmon. Fresh out of the water their colors are extraordinary, a subtle, complicated beauty of color impossible to describe, mottled and stippled—a background with colors of wet slate, with hues floating on it like the iridescent colors of oil on water, and stipples of a burning orange that is almost red, everything lightening toward the belly and suffused there with mottled deep pink, with maybe eight or so strange small circles of complicated color, targets or sunbursts an eighth of an inch in diameter containing five or six colors all subtly blending and super-imposed. The head is dark, like wet slate, egg-plant, black mushroom.

They weren't biting at the dam. I only got one, about eight inches. Charlie got one. Dick and George got twenty-three between them. Those twenty-three were laid out in descending size on the counter by the sink, an appealing sight (a custom). Dick tried to give me some, but I succeeded in refusing, as I knew they really wanted to eat them—and don't usually share catches among themselves.

Aside from class, money, etc., I feel divided from them by the specialization of my interests, and by my obsessions, that divide me from everyone.

July 10

Working in the garden, overcome at the edges with weeds. Milkweed—indicative of sour soil—with its large pom-poms of flowerets. I hear a humming, like a large housefly vibrating with a bass voice instead of soprano, or like the humming of a small motor. It was a humming bird, only a few feet away, at one of the pom-poms. Opened its beak (like chopsticks) and removed something deftly (maybe the old casing) then closed its long beak into a sipping straw, or hypodermic needle, and foraged among the flowerets that had already opened, probing with rapid, wonderfully discriminating thrusts among the opened flowerets. Its wings were a fan-shaped blur, humming. It positioned itself in the air before each pom-pom, moving in almost rectilinear patterns, little straight-line darts, as if all its moves were those of a chess board—though in fact it made other moves too—but this was the effect of its positioning. Its wings held it securely at *a point in space,* a position—and from this one position it moved its head up to reach a slightly higher floweret, or to one side or the other (like a papoose in the air, on the back of an invisible mother). The little feet dangled, as if it were ready to rest on a twig, but were just dangling, supported in air by that humming blur of wings. Iridescent green above, mottled creamy below, actually a profusion of subtle gloss, with brilliant iridescent yellow gores at both sides of the throat, speckled minutely with other colors (an effect somewhat of fishscales). It rested a moment on a milkweed leaf, still beating its wings ("beating" is the wrong word, though that *is* what it's doing), but beating them more slowly, and the sound drops to a lower note. The leaf scarcely even trembled, this weight was so slight. Then it flew to a nearby wild apple tree and perched. Its flight was a graceful long flattened S-curve. Later it perched higher on the gray birch. And I saw one later, after the rain, on the road to the cabin, high in the air sipping raindrops from a maple leaf.

July 30

Picking blueberries on Porter Hill. Susie and Amy (just back from European puppet work) went first with Shem. Becky and I (and Sashka) went through the woods later and joined them.

The profusion of leaf has peaked, things are quieter, no longer bursting, humming, blooming (though there are plenty of mosquitoes

and deer flies)—all that fullness seems poised, balanced before beginning the decline into Fall. There hasn't been much rain for a month.
The small streams are simply beds of mud now. These shadowed places
are still soft enough to take the impression of a foot (deer, dog, man),
but aren't oozy. We went up around noon. Morning birdsong over
(liveliest at daybreak)—woods quiet.

Wonderful to walk along with Becky, who is such an archetype of
child and so distinctive. (All archetypes are distinctive—they don't
resemble *average* figures and are not the same as *representative* figures—
they are ideals based on the demands and hopes generated in the world
beyond the *class of things* they stand above but are identified with.) She is
vigorous—walks with a big strong stride, equips herself with a staff
picked up beside the path, has an altered plastic gallon milk container
tied round her waist to put berries in, plucks the end of a fern and
wedges it between ear and head, it sticks forward out of her straight
brown hair like a green feather. She's spunky, lively, sometimes combative, sometimes tender, always earnest and straightforward, never
devious or mean. She's like a life force. The other children always want
to be with her. She's shapely and will be good-looking, but her face is
usually plain-attractive, a little freckled, wonderfully interested and
appealing, sometimes of striking beauty, but usually plain.

The fields terribly overgrown with weeds, bushes, and seedling
trees. Meadowsweet, maple, poplar springing up and crowding out
the berries. Grasses, milkweed, ferns, poison ivy. In the upper field the
berries are small and the birches are scattered in clumps intermitted by
grass and weeds, so that one must move about a good deal and the
gathering is slow. The berries are larger and of a brighter blue in the
lower field, the sloping field.

Becky eats all her berries. Susie and Amy gather with concentrated
attention, but they chat with Becky with enjoyment.

Amy: "Where did you stay last night?"

Becky: "At Craigon's. We picked raspberries after our bike trip,
and we got soaked from head to foot. I mean head to toe. Mordecai
said he *didn't* get soaked because he was under some bushes."

Amy: "What did you have for supper?"

Becky: "Uh . . . we had . . . what did we have? Oh yeah! We had collard greens and spaghetti and vegetable soup."

Amy: "Did you all stay there?"

Becky: "Clarinda and me and Karen did, but Mordecai and Trudi went home. We played sardine."

Amy: "What's sardine?"

Becky: "Well you know Dylan's house has a little playroom, and we all slept in there."

Amy: "Sardine is when a lot of people scrunch in beside each other?"

Becky: "Yeah, it's sort of a pile. I mean you're really close—and you sleep that way."

(Later)

I: "Are you sure the dogs ate the berries?"

Becky: "Yeah. Sashka stuck her head in the bucket."

I: "Did you see her chewing and swallowing? Because I offered her some and she didn't eat them."

Becky: "I think so. Here Sashka! Here Sashka! Look! *See! She's eating them!* What did I tell you!"

[NEIGHBORS]

MR. FIFE

I hadn't seen him for several months. It was the second of two mis-
placed hot summer days. I parked by the blacksmith (welding) shop.
His black German Shepherd, always chained by the doghouse, barked
and he came out. We shook hands and I said, "How've you been?"

"I'm just getting out of bed. I had flu twice. I was sick fourteen
days the first time and eleven the second. I got up too soon, that's what
the trouble was. Yeah. I said, 'Gee, I better get up and work or I never
will,' so I cut a whole line of poplars up in there, over there by the
birches. I shouldn't have done that. Oh, I was so weak. I had to send
for the doctor again. He wanted me to come to the hospital. I said *No
sir—right here!* Yessir. That's the first thing they say these days. Come to
the hospital. By gurry, if you haven't got somethin' when you go in,
you will after you've been there a while. Oh! Hey! Was that a bee? Oh!
Yes! . . . There he goes! Yeah, sure it's a bee. I'll have to write that
down. Those are Pike's bees. They come right over the hill there, from
Voter Hill. He's got about twenty hives. He used to have forty-five,
but there's so much traffic here . . . it kills them, you know. I used to
keep a couple myself, but the cars kill them. They ought to slow it
down. It's crazy. Of course it is! Forty miles an hour around that curve.
It doesn't make sense. And the bees can't survive it. They go down to
the strawberry fields, and then, you know, there's more traffic than
ever. The bees can handle it up to about twenty miles an hour. It's

mostly the young ones that die. They're tryin' out their wings. Sometimes I put honey out for them. I keep two or three pounds for that . . . entice 'em to the plants I want pollinated. I just spread it around near the plant, and don't you worry, they'll be up there in the plants soon enough. I always do that with the Greek leeks. No, no . . . these are one season leeks. They get this high (between knee and waist) . . . they're not just *leeks*, they're Greek leeks. That's where they come from . . . Greece, except I had to get the seeds in England. They won't send the plants, you know. These make bulbs. I'll give you some seed. Only don't use fertilizer! Here, look what I use . . ."

At the end of his garden was a small, neat compost pile. He pulled aside a top layer of leaves and brush and reached down to the bottom. He held a handful for me to look at. It was moist, crumbly, soft, black.

"That's it! That's right. It's compost. I use hen dressing—but it's three years old. When it's green, you know, it's twelve and a half percent nitrogen, and that's too much. It'll kill the roots. Yessir, it'll burn 'em. I've got another compost bin on the other side. Well, yes, you can bet the leeks like it. And don't I like the leeks! Ho ho. I wouldn't be without 'em! I'll give you some seed."

His garden is ahead of others. The Greek leeks—from seed he got from Greece via England, where he has relatives—were planted last August ("I planted those August 16th. The asparagus seed went in the 19th.") The leeks are ten inches high and he has already harvested some tops. "Ohhh! Are they good! Mmmm!! You cut them off about here—so they'll keep growing, see? Then you put them in a frying pan with some water and cook them till the water evaporates, about five minutes. Then you put some good dairy butter with them—not oleo, I've tried them both, the oleo is no good, use dairy butter. Then just fry them till they turn brown. Oh! My, are they good!"

"Flounder! Ohhh . . . isn't that good! You bet your life! Yessir! Togue I don't like too much—too fat. Give me a trout between six and eight inches, or white perch. A good white perch is the closest thing to flounder. But flounder! I clean it up good, scale it, get the fins and head off. Put some butter, real dairy butter, don't use margerine—

put some in with your cooking oil. Oh mister! Let me tell you! When that butter starts bubbling up around the fish! Ohhh . . . This time of year is a good time for them. We always brought some back. And I had a neighbor who used to go to the coast a lot. He'd say, 'If you hear a noise late at night, that's your fish.' He'd leave them on the doorstep in a box. He was a bachelor, so he kept his own hours. Freeze it in water. Put a little salt on it the day before and let it stand. Freeze it with the salt right on it."

His chives looked good too. "When they blossom you want to take the blossoms off—but don't throw them away! No sir! They're delicious. Eat them raw, just the way they are, in a sandwich.

"That's curly mint. That's catnip. Oh, that makes a delicious drink. And now's the time to pick it. People think they'll wait till fall, it's bigger—but they're wrong, it's no good then. Now's the time. Yessir. Just hang it up three or four days, then put it in a jar and keep it tightly covered. *Tightly* covered, see? Then just use it like tea leaves whenever you want it. Ohh, now, that's a good drink. Use the curly mint the same way. Do you have curly mint?"

Long frame of plastic on wooden frame, foot high, foot wide. "Couldn't you get the ground just as warm with a sheet of black plastic?" "No sir! I've tried them both. This is much better."

Showed me leeks, asparagus, strawberry ("I lost a lot this winter"), gave me young shoots of strawberry rhubarb grown from seed.

The tomatoes were in pots he'd made of sections of sewer pipe (black plastic). I said, "You made those out of sewer pipe," and he grinned and (characteristically) praised himself. He was now kneeling at the cold frame working with the tomatoes. "I've had two cutworms. Well, one was definitely a cutworm. The other I don't know."

Two kinds of tomatoes. "These are tree tomatoes. They grow high and they bear heavy. I had fifty-nine plants last year and I harvested one thousand three hundred and twenty-nine pounds of tomatoes. I sold a lot of them right across the road to Pike there. He wanted them all, but I said, 'Nossir! I have customers,' old people who can't do for themselves, and they come to me at night—not in the daytime. I'm too busy, I tell them; at night, at night's the time. And they take a bushel or two and can them. I freeze them myself. Oh they make good soup then, and good stewed tomatoes. And I freeze a lot of tomato juice. I put it in milk cartons. They're perfect for it. They expand when it freezes. Oh yes. That's the first thing I have, all winter. Tomato juice. I warm it up. Yes, that's the way to do it. Ohhh, that hits the spot.

"There used to be twenty-three canneries right here in this area. And there used to be grist mills. If somebody would start one of those up again, there'd be business for him. Sure there would. With grain the way it is? Ohh . . . you bet! They were common in Rhode Island when I was a boy. Oh yes, I used to walk along the river and study them. There was one I really liked the looks of. The wheel floated on pontoons so even when the water was low, it kept turning. The Temple sawmill you're talking about could only run in flood time. Sure, you could put a reservoir on top of a hill and let it down a sluice and run a mill—but don't pump it up there with a windmill. Use a ram. Do you know how they work?" (Diagram in pencil on the painted fence around the tomatoes.)

Mr. Fife II

When he sees the car, he comes running out alertly, eagerly, but not without territorial pugnacity—altogether like some sort of energetic, dauntless terrier or pit bulldog.

Wears an orange, visored cap—hunter's cap. Heavy, rubber-bottomed snowmobile boots, wool khaki pants (like old army pants), wool shirt, vest or sweater, hooded cotton jacket. It's quite cold (10°) and windy, but he seems snug. His eyeglasses and quick, small eyes, his broad cheekbones, sharply tapering chin, strong large nose (Indian, Scot), his long orange tusks—lower canines, gap between them.

He impresses me as being remarkably symmetrical, equal on both sides of a center line, balanced. You would even expect him to be ambidextrous. Thought becomes action immediately.

"Ohhh! You know I was expecting someone just this minute, I thought it was him!" Laughs. In high good spirits immediately. "Yeah, it's that fellow that plows the nurses' home. Did you know there's a nurses' home right next to the old hospital in that brick building? I didn't know that. Well . . . yeah . . . he broke his plow so I said I'd accomodate him and fix it. I don't know what his name is . . . *Paul*. I knew him when he was about that high, but twenty years go by and you don't recognize them. He said, 'I'm the one with red hair, do you know me now?' And I said, 'No mister, I sure don't.' Ha. Well how was the trip?"

I said: airport delays, wanted to get back, had been enjoying fishing, mistake to go but had been invited, tents and sleeping bags at Heathrow, French air controllers rule-book strike. "I'd've been better off staying here, I was enjoying it, but some friends invited me. . . ."

"Yeah . . . that's it . . . the same thing here, but I didn't go. I could have gone to Florida and California, free of charge. My old boss from Bar Harbor showed up one day with his wife. Well, I hadn't seen them years. 'We're goin' to Florida,' they said, 'you come with us.' 'Well, wait a minute,' I said, 'you just don't pull up and go.' 'We'll give you time,' they said. You know, they called me every two days. But it just didn't ring right. I didn't go. If I was to go anywhere it'd be Australia and New Zealand. My wife's people are down there. She used to try to get me to go. She said, 'I want you to meet them,' but I never did go. They're after me now . . . but no . . . I don't know . . . I like it here. . . ."

"If I could close this road off I'd have a greenhouse. But they're going to put the sewer line right underneath here. They want to run it from Temple Stream right up to the hospital. Now can you guess what it will cost? Just guess. Yessir! You got it. Two hundred thousand!"

"Did I show you the brackets I made? Come here, let me show you. . . ." We go to the little workshop across the road. So much iron and steel! It's not far from being a block of iron and steel!—tools, strips, rolls, etc. ("Mild steel is particles, forged in layers.") Shows me the brackets for kerosene lamps. Antique dealer wants them. "I'll sell the three together for a hundred. . . ." Shows me antique andirons he's repaired. Talk of antiques. Crooked dealers. Strap hinges (new) pickled overnight in brine. "He would leave them outside by the shop. A customer would see them: 'Oh . . . what are those old hinges out there?' 'Old hinges, huh? Well, I just found out they're worth something, I'm going to bring them in!' Yeah! Isn't that something? *Crooked?* Oh! When I gave him the new hinges, he said, 'I'll take a hammer and pound the shit out o' them.'" Fife mentioned a local dealer and made a face of disapproval and shook his head.

His wife had known something about antiques. He said he had just sold several old pieces to a dealer from Pittsfield.

I had gone over to get the leek seeds (from Greece via England. He said they were one-season leeks. I've needed two years for mine.)

"Hang them upside down. When they lose all green and the seeds are black under the skin, then plant them. About ten days from now. Here, this one's still good to eat. Look how green it is! Just smooth it up a bit. You have a little wooden mortar? That's it, then.

"I'll tell you a good way to do it. Take a brown paper bag, just a small one, and tie it over the head, see—then hang it upside down. When it's all dried out, you can just shake it and the seeds will end up in the bag. You've got enough there in those two heads to make two beds of leeks. Yessir! You'll be surprised."

"We had raspberries up the hill there. We let people come in and pick. Of course my wife could surprise them. When the bears got in there—I think there were three bears, not just one—they ruined it, they ruined next year's crop as well . . . oh it was just matted down and tangled. . . ."

We talked about bear, how they damaged a raspberry patch, how fast they could run ("but only a short distance"). "There used to be a slaughter house right up the hill here. We could hear 'em at night— aoooouuuu . . . Ha! ha! I thought, ohhh I'm going to get that bastard. I never did, though. They're clever, you know. And I didn't really have the time. Do you know what I saw once? and I've never forgotten it, it was so moving. I was out hunting and I came on a bear caught in a trap. I had my gun. Do you know what he did when he saw me coming at him? He covered his eyes with his paws. Just like this. I couldn't shoot him. I couldn't make myself do it. I told my wife about it. I knew who set the traps. He said they do it all the time. He was used to it, you see. He shot them. And he went around his line twice a day, yessir. Some trappers will let the animals sit for days. With beaver it's okay. They drown and they say that's not painful, for human beings, either. I guess it's not so good along the way, but they say it's not a painful death.

"I trapped beaver for three years. I used to weight my traps so they'd drown right away and not suffer. And if I knew there were a lot of young ones, I'd check the traps twice a day. But I used to trap the bank beavers. Those are the bachelors, you know. They live by themselves. And they're big, oh yes—you better believe it. I was out fox hunting once with my dog Popeye and he started after something. I thought, maybe it's a coon. But it was one of those bank beavers. He pulled it right out of the hole by its nose and I was ready. Wham! Yes sir! You don't want to shoot them. Oh no. That ruins the pelt. No sir. Right across the head with a club."

SHINERS ON HOOK WITH RUBBER BANDS

"All my secrets."

"Has to be a small one, that catches them right behind the gill. Big one won't work. I used to get them from the postman. Ha! Yeah. He said, 'You must use a lot o' these!' Yeah! Oh I do! I do! I put a fresh one on each time, you see. It gets loose if you don't. Oh, it works like a charm. Shiner lasts a lot longer. Wags his tail so good. Yeah." (Shows me with finger.)

Me: "What way does the barb face?"

"Here's your hook. . . ."

"So the shiner faces your rod?"

"Yeah, that's it."

MR. FIFE III

His violent watch dog rushes out of its house (a traditional dog house) and dashes as close to me as his chain will allow, barking fiercely. Mr. Fife comes out spryly. "Hush up! Get back in there."

The dog is always chained—and actually somewhat expresses Mr. Fife's relation to the world, i.e., embattled, surrounded by a strong fortress, protected by caution, sagacity, competence. He is a gifted, rather wonderful crank, full of energy, enjoyment, self-appreciation and remarkable competence in many things. But he thinks the rest of mankind are ninnies.

"Kids don't like to work today. I don't know what it is. They get driven around, they get entertained. I thought I'd hire the Buckley boys, right up here in West Farmington, to help me in the garden a while. Well, you know when they came they had a note from their father—*pay these boys one fifty an hour.* Can you beat that? He didn't even know what work they'd be doin'! *Pay these boys* . . . well by gurry I sent 'em right home with a note of my own said, *Put 'em to work. Yessir.*

"When I was a boy (Rhode Island), I had chores to do after school. And we didn't get bussed to school. And we didn't walk, either, we ran! Yessir! And when I got home, I went right to the coal shed and brought in the coal. Every day. And every other day I filled the wood bin. We had a bin you could fill from the outside. It held enough for two days. And then maybe I'd run to the store for groceries. Today if a woman wants a loaf of bread, she jumps in the car and drives five miles to get it. You talk about energy saving! What does that loaf of bread cost by the time you figure it up? And it's the same way with farming. Listen, you know Whalen, has that nice herd of Black Angus by the river in New Sharon? Eight years ago, before he got 'em, he talked with me, and I said, *You can make money if you're self-sufficient, otherwise you'll lose it.* Yessir. That's what I told him. *If you can't grow your own feed, don't do it.* Well, he grows his own feed. And the price of beef has gone up and up. And you know, his wife called me this winter. She said, *Everything you predicted has come to pass!* Yessir! Well . . . of course . . . I love farming. There's nothing like it in the world. I love it. If I was a hundred-fifty years old I'd still be farming. . . ."

MR. FIFE IV

Mr. Fife was splitting the oak with a big axe. Energetic, talkative— actually elated.

"Some of it splits easy and some splits hard. This one here was right on the line where a lot of pine was cut. So it caught a lot of wind. It twisted, you know (does it with his hands, whole body)—*sure*, that made it tough.

"Here, look here. This is a cross between a pin oak and a red oak. I root pruned it to stunt it." He braces himself in a bowlegged, almost squatting stance, imitating the stunted oak. His speech is rapid, detailed and expressive, and his body is part of it. He acts things out, makes innocent, ironic, mocking, outraged, wisely scornful faces, pokes me to prod the proper amused connivance—and I feel his strength, that very short but sturdily made, muscular body, with just the beginning of softness in the lower gut, no pot belly at all—and he bawls me out by saying, "If you'd cut your own wood and stop being so lazy, you wouldn't have that belly. I use a buck saw on almost everything, and a crosscut saw. I only use the chain saw if it's too big."

The oak: "I was walking with my wife and we came through a stand of red oak, and up ahead I could see there was a lot of pin oak, and by gurry, right in the middle was a little tree that was a cross. I said, 'Look at this! We'll take it home!' This is it! Yes! That was thirty-five years ago. I fed it well until it got established, then I root pruned it. What do we need a big tree for? No. This is perfect. Look! Look at the acorns. You see? They're shaped like the red oak acorns, but they're short. Oh, don't the squirrels love them! You should've seen the squirrels that were here a few days ago. Oh! There were dozens of them! Now, see here where I pruned it. Look, you see how the tree has healed. Look! The bark is pulled across just so neat! Yessir! I was trained by a man who knew his stuff. He spent his whole life at it, not like these young guys who go around and try to do the whole thing in one step. What's the name of those tree people? No, no—I mean the ones that cut for the town. Well, I forget his name, but he came around just after I cut that limb. Now the secret is—I'm telling you part of the secret—you leave about two inches of the limb, you don't cut it flush. Yessir! That's the trick! But do you think they know that? Don't you believe it! No sir! That young fellow came by and said, 'Oh, you didn't do that right. You should've cut it flush.' And I said, 'Oh, is that the way it's done? You cut it flush? Well I'm happy to learn that.' See? I didn't say a word. Now I'll tell you the second part of the secret. Listen to this now. After the wood in that two-inch stump is all dried out, and the sap has pulled back into the tree—*then* you cut it flush, and you paint it up good with that tree tar. Look. You see? Perfect healing! The bark covers it up again right to the center. Now do you think that young man ever saw a cut like that? No sir! How could he? Where would he see it? They're in a hurry. They want to do it all at once and move on. Well, when I saw it was healed, I called him over one day and I said, 'How do you like the looks of *that*!' 'Well I'll be damned. Well I'll be damned.' 'Yessir, you'll be damned for a fool, because you don't know your business!' Don't you forget, mister, I was a nurseryman for forty-five years. We had the filling station, the nursery, and the welding. Yessir, everything I have I made by the sweat of my brow. We weren't afraid of work. When we came back from the coast with fish, we stayed up till they were in the freezer. I mean fifty or sixty pounds of fish. Same with the planting. When the time was right, we did it. We didn't do a little now and a little then and lay around and get tired. We *did* it. Why, we used to ship a hundred and twenty-five thousand pine seedlings a year.

That's not a lot. Started them all from seed right here. Do you know that fellow out in Strong . . . what's his name now? . . . the one with the tree farm. That was put in thirty years ago. He came to me and said, 'I've got the seedlings and a crew, but we don't know how to do it. Can you show us how?' Oh yes, he had a crew all right. They were terrible. They could do a row or two, but they couldn't keep going (he wipes his brow, rolls his eyes, wilts). And they thought they were planting trees just because they put them in the ground! No sir! That's not planting. You do *this* . . . (He paces off a hefty yard with his short legs, pushes the imaginary dibble, stamps firmly with one foot north and west, with the other south and east, and strides off another yard, every movement firm and rhythmic.) I said, 'Send the crew home, I can do it faster myself.' I did too. And I told him, 'That's mighty poor stock you're planting. If you want to see good stock, you come with me.' But he said, 'Oh this will grow'—Fat chance! Half of it *didn't* grow. There's lots to learn. You can't just plant the trees and come back in thirty years. If you want first-class wood, you want to prune the trees while they're young. Most people wait, or don't do it, then the trees have knots. And they're big ones.

"I'm going to cut my oak grove soon. Half of it. And I'll scale every stick that leaves it. You bet I will. It's too valuable.

"What? You have 500 acres of wood and you cook with gas! Poo! Shame!"

"Of course this oil shortage is phony! There's no shortage! They've got that stuff stored away till the price is right. Ohhh . . . they're so crooked . . . so crooked . . . Every time that Carter opens his mouth I see another five cents on the gas pumps. And what about that Ford? Do you think he'll die a poor man after pardoning Nixon? Oh I guess not! Here. Let me show you this. I think I have it in my wallet. Just wait now, just wait, oh it's good. I wrote Jack Anderson, you know, at the time of Spiro Agnew, and I got an answer. Here it is. Now. Here. Look at this." (Clipping) "And I found out Spiro was a Mason, a top Mason. Are you a Mason? Stay away from those guys."

DICK BLODGETT II

He came to look at the barn. One post has been settling and needs to be jacked up.

"Aren't they nice barn boards! They've weathered nicely."

I mentioned that the new dog Woody, a Bernese Mountain Dog, shy of adult males, hadn't barked and run at him. As usual Dick responded in such a way as to imply that there was no basis for a compliment. "I've always been shy of dogs and horses. I've been kicked so many times by horses—not by dad's (we did everything with them, oh sure, we lumbered and ploughed and hauled) but I worked lots with horses that weren't clever. . . ."

We were standing inside the barn. "One of dad's last horses ended its days right here. He sold it to old Vic, but with the understanding that Vic would lay him away when he began to go down, and not sell him again. Dad was funny about that. Some of the old timers here were quite mean to their horses. If there was a bit of work left in it, they'd try to get it. Dad didn't want any horse of his worked to death. He'd rather see them laid away."

I took him to see the corner garden that I'd just weeded and thinned—corn, with a patch of potatoes, and one of beans, and one of pumpkins and squash. Mabel had planted all of it. It looked very pretty after the rain. The corn was about a foot high.

"Everything's so late this year because of that spell of rain. I couldn't plough for the longest time. Didn't it stay wet! The corn looks good. You've got a lot of it. We used to say, *Knee high by the fourth o' July*— but these late gardens always catch up, they make it. Weren't the birds bad this year! It's the starlings more than the crows. They'll pull everything up when it's about this high (three-four inches). Yours is safe now. And mine made it all right. But Charlie Lilja's field was wiped out. He plants up at my place. The two fields are side by side, and his was torn up completely and mine wasn't touched. I heard that starlings are afraid of snakes so I got some old wire and BX cable and made a lot of snakes and set them out in the corn. Must work! Every few days I'd move them around. And I heard something I'm going to try in the fall against the coons. We have a terrible time with them. They usually get most o' the corn. And last year they did lots of damage in the pear trees. The boys shot four in one tree one night. They got most of the pears and broke a lot of branches. I don't know what to do about that, but I'm going to try Rotenone on the corn tassels. They say the coons hate the taste of it. And it's safe. It breaks down quickly in the weather, and the corn silk keeps growing out anyway.

A long conversation about health. His wife Helen's three operations for tumors, all fortunately benign.

"You know I'm getting on. I'm fifty-nine. I've had angina attacks lately—if I lift too much. I was mixing cement the other day, not that I had to, but I was helping out. Why, that would've been nothing to me at one time, but now it's too much. Dad had angina too."

I say: should get EKG, etc.

"I used to go once a year for a check-up, but I haven't been in for years. Anything they might tell me would be bad news . . . and I don't know . . . I'd just as soon not hear it."

I asked him in for a drink. "Or are you still on the wagon?"

"Oh no. I'm drinking again. Not like I was. . . . "

Me: "You're not supposed to give it up entirely. They just found out that drinkers have fewer heart attacks than non-drinkers. They're quoting this Scandinavian cross-country skier. He's 104 and still skiing. He says 'Get lots of exercise and don't drink too much. But don't drink too little, either.' They recommend two shots a day."

"That's nice advice!"

I mentioned the bookcase-cabinet. He: "Well . . . I've got it cut out. I don't know. It's just like writing. You have to be in the mood to do that kind of work, especially after all this rough stuff I've been doing."

"Dana (five or six, his grandson) and I picked a quart and a half of wild strawberries. He loves to do it. He's a good berry picker. He said, 'Gramps, don't ever sell this place. When I grow up I want to pick the berries.' It's going to be a good berry year. Good apple year, too."

HORSESHOES

"No, we don't play for money. Nobody could beat me for money."

"Watch out now! When you play me you're playing a professional."

"Good shoe! Good shoe! Now if you can just get it in the box you'll be all right."

"You can't beat luck." (Larry's first shoe knocked Dick's ringer away from the stake. His second shoe was a ringer.)

(Larry's ringer) "Look at that! It hits the front o' the pit, digs up a stone in the middle, hits the back, bounces forward and he makes a ringer! You can't beat luck."

(My shoe went onto the road.) "We'll have to have 'em stop traffic while George throws."

Dick Blodgett III

Sunday (29 July) was Old Home Day at the Intervale Church. Dana was there, and his son. I asked if Dana's son was in good health.

"No, he's not. . . ."

"What's wrong with him?"

"Well, he's muddled in his head. I guess he always has been. It goes back a long way. He's been in the insane asylum several times. He's harmless, he's never done anything—but he's the kind of person you have to watch out for. He *could* do something. To talk to him he seems perfectly all right, he makes sense—but then every once in a while he goes off . . . ayeh . . . there's a pattern of it in the family . . . (he names others in Temple who had mental problems). Temple seems to have had more than its share of mental problems, I don't know why." Story of being a sign painter in psychiatric hospital in the army—painted signs directly on walls, or patients would use them as weapons. He was painting one day when "everything went flying. This patient had seen me standing there working and decided to tackle me. We wrestled for about an hour. I used to like to wrestle. And wasn't this guy strong! He wasn't as big as me, but my! he was strong. We got to be pretty good friends. His name was Dick too. A couple of months after that he escaped—and how he did it took amazing strength. . . ."

I went over to watch the Ali films on TV with Dick. George and Charlie were welding the frame of a trailer bed in the garage (two-wheeler, to be hauled by truck or car). I said, "What goes on there?" "Anything you want. This is going to get an old pick-up body."

The house and grounds are so attractive, cheerful and open—ample, generous, farm and home (even though not much farming is going on).

People are always coming around (many relatives in Temple—in-laws). Charlie has garden space there, and is frequently up there, often with his wife, working in the garden. George Blodgett's there almost every day, and his three sons are extremely fond of their grandad, and play there often. Dick stocked the pond with trout so they could fish.

Boxing talk while we watch the fight films.

"Of course Joe Louis was the one in my day. He fought everyone, just like Ali. I'd love to see that fight—Louis and Ali. . . ."

"I think Ali might have taken him. He was so much faster."

"Prob'ly would, yes . . . Henry Armstrong was my fighter. He held the championship in three weight divisions. I never thought too much of Dempsey. It was hard to tell about him.

"My game was pool. That's a wonderful game. I played for quite a few years. Nobody could beat me at that. Did you ever play that?"

VILIO

I stopped at Dick Blodgett's on the way home from the Orchard Hill Cemetery, where I had taken some rubbings.

Dick: "Isn't that too bad about Vilio. Did you hear about Vilio?"

Vilio was in Thayer Hospital in Waterville with a broken vertebra in his neck and a damaged shoulder. He had been felling trees in Dick's pine grove the day of the very high wind. He had finished cutting and was about to leave and was bending over to pick up his chainsaw, when the wind uprooted a good sized pine and it came down across his shoulder and neck.

". . . Boy that guy has bad luck. But of course if he'd've been standing he'd've been killed. Bad luck runs in that family. There've been more injuries and deaths. Bertha had a boy by another marriage and he was killed in an automobile accident. Then Vilio's sister was murdered by her husband, who went on and killed himself. And he's been banged up in the woods. He broke his hand and wrist a couple of years ago. And broke his leg before that. . . ."

I went to see Vilio the day after he got out of the hospital. Dick Blodgett was leaving just as I arrived. We talked briefly about the Christmas party at the Historical Society.

Vilio was sitting at the kitchen table wearing a neck brace and a light sling for his right arm. A man his own age sat in a chair by the wall. Weikko—as usual, anxious, tormented, angry, shy—stood leaning back against the stove with his arms folded.

Small talk. I had brought a couple of magazines and kidded him, saying that one of them would teach him how to play poker. He said he'd be laid up quite a while. It would be a few weeks before he could even hold the cards to play poker. "They say it might be five or six months before I can work again. And I have to keep this damn sling on for a while. But there's nothing I can do anyway, so I guess it won't be too hard."

About the accident: "I never saw what hit me. I woke up in the car on the way to the hospital. Toby and Charlie Lilja brought me in. You know, the doctor commended them. They saved my life. They realized I had a broken neck and they carried me just right, so my head wouldn't move, you know. They learned that in rescue techniques at the Fire Department. The doctor said it was lucky for me they were the ones to bring me in. He wrote them a note and left it with my clothes. But they wouldn't touch me at Franklin. They wanted a neurosurgeon, you know."

Vilio said all this in that factual, uncomplaining, innocent style of his. "I don't believe these young doctors know what they're doing today. They didn't do right by me when I broke my wrist. Went away on vacation and didn't leave me no pills or nothin', and the thing was infected. I had to go in again and get injections." He held out his left hand—a large hand, bony and sinewy, but not thick like Dick's hands, or Eddie's. Large knuckles, deformation in a couple of fingers, and the way it joined the wrist was not quite right. "This hand got pinched between two trees when they fell together. I can use it (flexing the fingers), but it never did heal right. It's half numb a lot o' the time. I have to be careful with it."

Vilio is rugged, but isn't powerful. Tim Jones, who'd worked with him for a while in the woods, said that he was a very smooth cutter, very efficient. But he has always had accidents. The best cutter around was the one who cut his leg off at the shin.

VILIO II

Talking about his elder son (at poker):

"Weikko's got eight stitches just above his eye here (shows, as always) . . . He cut a spring-pole." (A sapling or small tree bent to the earth by the weight of a larger tree, felled or windblown. These spring-poles have tension in them, and when they are cut straight across they split, and part springs erect with great force, enough to kill if the blow lands in the wrong place. The technique is to release the tension by cutting vertically, releasing a few fiber-bundles at a time.) "He saw it was there, and he cut it right. I mean he didn't go across on the damn thing. But you know what? That goddamn (he says *gaww-dam*) tree was twisted two different ways. Now who the hell can notice that kind o' thing? I mean you can't take the time to walk around every gaww-dam spring-pole an' figure it out. Hell. You wouldn't sell much wood."

VILIO III

"If you want me to show you where your lines are, I'll come over. I think I can still find 'em. I used to own that piece up there by your camp. I was born right in that house there. Oh yeah. That used to be a nice set o' connected buildings. I bought it from French and cut it, and sold it to Hoxie. He was the one that built the camp. Oh yeah . . . that used to be a nice farm there."

"I quit school to work in the woods. Times were tough then. I was fourteen. That was the Depression, you know. That was about 1933. You'd work up a whole cord o' wood, all split in four-foot lengths, for a dollar back then. I worked for my dad until I was seventeen. All the Finns were woodcutters back then, you know. But we kept some animals and hens, and that was half the living. Then when I was seventeen I thought, Jesus, I can't live here forever. Me and Taamo—you know Taamo, who died back here a couple o' months . . . yeah . . . oh, Jesus, that was too bad . . . he got the flu, you know, and didn't tend it. It deposited a lot o' fluid around his lungs. He collapsed on the floor there, but he told his mother what number to call, and the ambulance came and got him. Then the very next day he had a heart attack right there in the hospital. Oh, he was some athlete. He wasn't a big man, but *tough*. You should've seen 'im pitch. We had a ball team, you know, me and Dick and Larry and Bruce and Billy Mosher. We took almost everybody. Taamo used to strike out sixteen players. And that was after a day in the woods. Me and Taamo used to buddy around a lot. We went off and cut together in New Hampshire and Massachusetts. The pay was a lot better than around here. We worked good together. We used bucksaws and crosscut saws back in them days. Jesus, you get with the wrong man it'd feel like you were draggin' him back and forth with every cut. But me and Taamo, we could work all day long and not be tired, and we'd cut five cord o' wood. It was all rhythm, you know. We was neither one very big, we weighed a hundred-fifty, a hundred-sixty pounds, but we was rugged. Toby is like that. Jesus that boy can work. He'll pick up a stick you wouldn't think he could lift, and by God if he don't pick it up no man will. He's got the gumption o' three men. I'll tell you that. The only thing about Toby is that damn heart, you know. He's got to have another operation sometime, one o' them plastic valves, but they say he oughta wait till the last minute to do it. It don't slow him down none, but it tires him out.

"When we got back from the service, we'd have to walk in and out a couple o' weeks at a time before they packed the roads. We'd use skis or showshoes. But there'd get to be a beaten trail and we'd just walk. The Finns was the only ones to use the skis. I don't know why, because they sure worked good. Taamo used to have that place that Bresloff has now (on top of a long and steep hill that ends abruptly at the road/store/stream) and he kept quite a few hens. He used to take two o' them *ten-quart* wire egg-baskets, one in each hand, and ski right down to the store without crackin' a one. And that weren't easy, havin' to stop at the bottom just by turnin' the skis in, you know, with nothin' but a strap holdin' your feet there. I guess the best skier around, even better than Taamo, was my half brother Oiva. He's not doin' too good these days—Jesus, he's only got an eighth of his stom-ach left."

To Dick (at poker): "The only time my neck don't hurt me is here at the poker game."

Larry: "Losing money relieves it, eh Vilio?"

George Blodgett: "All you gotta do is cut a hole in your pocket."

Vilio: "Well now, I don't see no big pile o' silver and green in front o' *you*. There's an awful lot o' table showin', if you ask me. Matter o' fact, I'm not doin' so bad."

Ronnie: "My whole pile's slid right over in front o' you. You sure you didn't tilt the table?"

Vilio: "Half your pile."

Larry: "An' half o' mine . . ."

Vilio: "You? You started out with half. . . ."

Charlie: "And it was all down hill from there."

Dick (dealing): "Well I'll give you another ace when I get to you, Barker."

Larry (receiving a four): "Is that your idea of an ace?"

Dick: "Next time. . . ."

Dick and Vilio had a stiff exchange about money. Vilio insisted that Dick was giving him too much for the cutting. He put the check in his pocket and gave Dick $25 cash from his wallet. Dick wouldn't take it. "No, no, what about those birch tops, that's firewood." "No sir, that's your money, I wouldn't charge you for that." "No, no, take it Vilio. Take it—put it in your pocket, it's yours." "No sir. I got mine in my pocket. That's yours," etc. George and I said nothing. "I got a feeling it's best to keep the hell out of this."

Vilio: "I don't want no tip or nothin'." "I know you don't, that's got nothin' to do with it." "That's your money." Dick relented rather than give serious offense.

BEN STAPLES

Ben Staples delivering mail—car full of groceries to take to elderly women along route. And would deliver messages. Also he carried pruning shears, saw, axe. "I hate to see these back roads get all overgrown, so I clear 'em out as I go."

An elderly lady would call Slim, who would put up the order at the store and give it to Ben.

People would meet him at the mailbox and chat for a while.

"Today nobody knows what a village was like."

One day, because of snow, he wasn't able to drive the mail route. He didn't have to go, but he decided he wanted to, and went on foot. "The only trouble was, by the end of the day I was so full of coffee and doughnuts I could hardly move."

ESTHER JOHNSON

Mabel drove me to Esther Johnson's house, which is on a ridge that parallels ours. There used to be a bridle trail through the woods that came out near our house, but I didn't know where it began and wanted to ask Esther.

Her land is the highest around. There are wonderful views in all directions, fields, wooded hills and clefts, though mostly wooded hills. Her land repeats the topography of the region in miniature—knobs and hills in all directions. There are thirty or forty apple trees, some rail corrals, in disrepair since there are no horses now. (Her daughter Tammy won hundreds of ribbons growing up.) The grass everywhere is nibbled short, and I've never seen it any other way, since she's always pasturing some sort of critter. In the sunny ell of the barn we could see a black yearling bull, and two younger ones from Jack's barn that she had taken over. "I don't know *what* was wrong. He fed them, they ran right along with the herd, but they were just rawhide and not much of it at that. They're coming along well now."

Her house is close to the road, with the land rising in back of it. The shed and large barn are attached to the house at right angles. Huge maples in the small front yard.

A plump woman in her middle sixties stood in front of the house. She wore baggy, nondescript slacks and a discolored, dirty, lavender-colored shirt that was almost a tunic. Her hair was a pale red and stood out from her head all around, yet did not have much body to it. Her face was pleasant and friendly. She recognized Mabel. "Esther's in the barn," she called, "we had triplet kids last night. Would you like to see them? Be careful. The surface of the ground is terribly slippery." She spoke with exaggerated courtesy, an almost courtly style. At first it was pleasant, but within a few minutes it began to seem mannered and egotistical, especially in comparison with Esther's wonderfully intelligent, candid, luminous style that is actually noble. Only Florence Blodgett, who at eighty-two is ten years her senior, has a comparable graciousness; but her style is more lady-like than Esther's—and Esther is not gracious, or is not aware that she is, but graciousness, or maybe grace, is almost a by-product of the intersection of other virtues. She is endlessly generous, compassionate, forgiving. Many people depend on her and tend not to offer much help, and she never fails them. She has great immediacy, is always present, in her skin, is never preoccupied but always actively busy.

Mabel: "Is it unusual to have triplets?"

Plump Woman: "No, I wouldn't say so. But it's a goodly number. Esther! Your friends are here. . . ."

We passed through part of the barn—an organized clutter too complex even to register on a brief glance. Through another board door we came to a low-ceilinged area of stalls. Several dogs began to bark.

Esther greeted Mabel with affectionate matter-of-factness—a laconic greeting inserted into a flow of practical comment, but their hands managed to touch and hold each other a brief moment. I was saddened to see how Esther has aged. I hadn't seen her for several years.

She wore brown slacks, work boots, a man's shirt of a cream color—yet the effect was not mannish, but practical. She has always worn her hair short. She's a middle size, neither sturdy nor frail, but capable-looking and active. She has a long, intelligent, English face, a noticing, reflective face. On both sides of the little central aisle there were stalls and cages. Goats in the stalls and dogs in the cages. One of the goats had only one foreleg—a knee-length stump dangled beside it. "The Llasa-Apsos got to it one night and chewed the leg right off the poor thing." Esther has been breeding and raising dogs for many years—small ones exclusively, since the big ones eat too much. All the Pugs in Temple are from litters of hers. She runs ads in the dog magazines and occasionally sells to dealers.

The goats really seemed like exotic creatures, desert animals living most artifically in Maine. Their bulging eyes are very close to the tops of their heads, like the eyes of camels. They are all bulges and bony leannesses. The three kids, less than twenty-four hours old, were frisking in a tentative, wobbly, uncoordinated way, yet were frisking. Their coats were as soft as fine velvet. One was spotted, black and white, the others were streaked black and a dark soft gray. Esther bent down and went through the tiny door into their stall. "I can't do this so well anymore, I'm getting old." She brought out one of the kids and held it in her arms stroking it, so we could see it closely. "That's the mother right there. No, it's not good to let them nurse their kids. I'll put the kids on a bottle. It ruins the udders, I don't know why. I let that brown one there nurse her kids for a few weeks and she developed ulcers. I cleared them up all right, but it took a while."

The little dogs on both sides—also nursing litters—were rearing against their cages (chicken wire) and barking. This barking wasn't like the barking you hear in pet shops. Esther treats them all extremely well. She talked to them and petted them while we were there.

There are dogs in the house, too. She told us how one of them, a mixed Corgi and Chihuahua, had killed the pups of the Pug in the adjacent cage just last night while the goats were being born. "She's a nice dog, she's affectionate, she's wonderful with children, she's smart as can be, but she's done this before. I'll have to get rid of her. She's wonderful with her own pups, but the pups of other dogs . . . well, I don't know, she just has to kill them. I didn't punish her, there's no point in that. She doesn't know what she's doing, it's an instinct that comes from deep down. But I'll have to find a home for her, and if I can't find one I guess I'll put her to sleep."

Esther invited us into the house to meet her son, who lives with his family thirty miles away and who comes to help her when something special needs to be done. We passed through the large woodshed. There were still several tiers of split stove wood, good sized chunks. A heavy axe was sunk in the chopping block, a section of maple trunk, and I guessed it was her son who used it.

Esther's daughter, Tammy, is a rural hippie. Eight years ago she married an eccentric, gifted, bushy-headed youth who had come here from some city or other. He did nothing but play the guitar and lay around. But apparently he played with real originality, and was known to a small number of people, some of whom would travel a long way to come play with him. Then he stopped playing. They live in a small cabin not far away, with a couple of children. He has picked up wood lore and now makes a living as a trapper. His younger brother, with the same bushy reddish-brownish blonde hair, and the same slow, lazy, yet energized and strangely attractive manner, has been visiting, or hanging around, for several months, a good bit of the time with Esther. He was standing at the big cookstove (wood) in the kitchen, barefoot, frying a piece of bread. Esther introduced us. Both Mabel and I had seen him before in town, had mistaken him for his brother and so had spoken with him. He smiled brightly, actually with a lot of contact, but said nothing. One imagines that he'll "emerge" at some point, maybe in ten years.

Esther kept up a running conversation, all informative, feelingful, succinct. Her ancient, ancient aunt had been living with her, but the doctor had insisted she go to a nursing home. Neither Esther nor her sister (the plump woman) was strong enough to pick the woman up if she fell, or lift her to a bed pan. "It's a nice enough home," said Esther, "but those are terrible places, so many old people all there together. The last time we went out one of the women was screaming, and others were crying. Ethyl cried all the time we were there, just silently, you know."

Ten years ago Esther took in young boys from the state as a foster parent, and has also done the same with elderly people.

Her son was not in the house. He had come with her brother to fix the line from the spring, which had frozen at one of the fittings in the spring.

The house was cluttered, somewhat odorous, heavily used, repaired, patched, the usual signs of poverty with far more than the usual signs of use.

Esther picked up some dog shit in a paper towel and threw it in the parlor wood stove. Her sister had walked right by it. Esther said, without reproach, "She's just like me, she goes right by it and doesn't see it."

Here in the parlor were two dog cages. In one was a Pug, with only two pups; in the other, facing it, was the puppy-killing Corgi-Chihauhau. Esther said of the Pug, "Those aren't her pups. She grieved so over the dead ones, I went and got her these. She kept licking them, trying to revive them, and getting frantic."

We went outside and climbed the handsome hill. It was a beautiful day. We passed a large, tarpaper shack. An elderly man lived there, younger than Esther and in good health. He had made an agreement to help with the chores in lieu of payment for food and rent. But he had stopped helping a long time ago. Esther had asked him to leave, but he wouldn't, and she hadn't pressed the matter. "He means well enough, I suppose," she said, "but he drinks, you know. Cecil (her son) says I should throw him out, but I don't know where he'd go. I'm too soft-hearted I guess."

From the top of the hill we could see two men on the far side coming towards us.

Esther's son was in his early forties, large and strong and pleasant looking. Her brother, coming some distance behind, red-faced and panting, was exceedingly ugly. His body was very large and shaped like a barrel, though rather more bulgy in the middle. His face was bloated, of bad color and texture. He looked like a heavy drinker and as if he might possibly have a bad, bad temper.

Cecil said they had repaired the fitting and put new insulation on the spring cover. We chatted very briefly. Esther's brother said to her, jocularly but rather heavily, "Just don't get in my path this morning. I might run you down. I might put my boot on your punkin' head and crush it right into the ground." He smiled and glanced at us. Esther didn't smile, didn't reprove him, but started back toward the house, going at a good pace, as she always does. In the house she told me how to find the trail. Mabel and I chatted a bit more with her and then left.

But Esther hadn't been up that way, obviously, in several years. The road had been pushed another mile into the woods, and there were several new cabins along it. I came out just above my cabin instead of just below the house.

That night I walked through the flood to go to the weekly poker game. The water had dropped a good three feet, but there was still a long puddle of foot-deep water in the low place. Waves preceded me as I strode through it, and in the waves the reflections of the stars swayed wildly, and the straight lines of the trees buckled and quivered. Orion was very low in the west.

Some talk at the game of roads washed out, and talk of spring mud:

Vilio: "Bertha says (of Hervey, the young Road Commissioner) he's always worrying about getting signs on the roads so people won't get stuck, but he's always the one who gets stuck."

Vilio drove me to my road after the game. We talked about playing poker and shooting dice in the army and navy.

"I never liked dice," he said, "I never really understood it and it goes so fast, you know. But I had good luck at poker. I came home with some money. I had enough to buy that place. That was before I knew Bertha."

I waded through the water again and went very amblingly up the road. It was brisk, but not really cold—about one in the morning. I'd had four beers and a long parting slug of vodka and felt good.

SOFTBALL

In the field by the old school house, now the town meeting house.

A lumber truck booms by, piled high with stout, eight-foot bolt wood. The horn. A heavy arm thrust from the window waves. Several of the players wave back, and a couple shout.

"Good fire! Good fire! Take it to him, Big Ken. Good whip!"

"I heard it hit somebody and I got all set to hurt, then I realize it was you."

A pickup truck goes by. Waving again.

The field: the green back of trees, the brown canvas backstop, the green grass, thick, very green, the reds and blues against it, and sunburned torsos, bare legs, red and white socks, blue jeans, caps of all colors. Wives and children on benches on two sides. Bare torsoed umpire. Coolers of beer in both camps.

"Close the cooler! Close the cooler! Never mind his fractured skull, cover the beer!"

"That your medicine chest?"

"You got it!"

They shake hands immediately and with real warmth at the final out—with such alacrity and feeling that one could almost imagine that the entire game had been a prelude to this.

SOFTBALL II

Canvas back-stop on posts that not too long ago were young trees. The field bounded on two sides by woods—the ball rolls from the grass into a thin strip of ferns and bushes, and then among trees, seedlings, and saplings. It is not easy to find when it's fouled badly and comes down from a high arc into the woods. The road on one side, the meeting house ("town hall") on the other, that once had been the school.

There are benches to the left and right of the batter's box. Players occasionally sit there, but most of the space is taken up by wives and children and girlfriends, though mostly wives. Two or three elderly, and maybe three or four others have brought folding chairs, which they set up in the grass near the trucks and cars that are parked in the long driveway that encircles the meeting house.

The warm-up, beginning to "talk-it-up." The visiting team (a company team—but this means that many of the young men of a small, but not tiny, town have been candidates, from which the best have been selected) wear uniforms, but our home team is playing in whatever.

First inning. Our home team in the field talks it up energetically, and the energy rises, excitement is generated.

"Come right to 'im, buddy, come right to 'im!"

"Come on, big Red, come on big Red!"

"Good eye, Larry, good eye!"

"Smoke 'im out! Smoke 'im out!"

"Good arm, Eddie! Good arm!"

"No problem, Weikko! No sweat! No sweat!"

"Way to go, John! Way to go!"

Elderly couple in folding chairs, flapping their hands at the black flies and mosquitoes, and then a large wasp begins to buzz them. The man gets up to kill it, but has trouble locating it; the woman turns in her chair. A young woman comes by carrying a child's sweatshirt she has fetched from the family truck, and seeing their problem goes to them with a big smile, locates the wasp, smacks him with the sweatshirt, peers into the tall grass where he has fallen and stomps him with one vigorous, decisive stomp of her boot. She turns to the elderly couple and grins, they smile at her, she continues on to one of the benches by the backstop, where her child is waiting for his sweater, and where she'll sit and drink a beer and watch her husband and his teammates.

"Play the stick! Play the stick!" (Two outs, a man on first—advice from the fielders' coach—but the play is a force at second.)

The game is even for a while, though the visitors have more quality at every position. The inner superiority finally bursts out in the fourth inning. Our pitcher makes an error in a throw to first; two more errors and bad throws and suddenly the score is seven to one.

The players' physiques, styles, characters:

Their first-baseman—strong, red-headed, a good athlete, body oriented to his hips, a graceful slouch, resting, leaning back, his hips thrust forward, a fast runner and good at catching and throwing, confident and lending confidence to others, not strong at bat. Courteous, tough, virile, respectful of others and demanding respect, slow to speak criticism, but not slow to notice the things that deserve it.

Our first baseman—wide, heavy-boned frame, strong strong back, huge belly still riding high in his early thirties, but so large that it impedes his play, though he is deft. Strong bass voice and active use of it encouraging his teammates. Sullen round face, new beard.

POKER

Ages 63, 60, 60, 35, 30, 53, all married men with children.

Dullness, narrowness of life, appalling sameness of days, disappointment, desperation, traces of bitterness, stirrings of a rage that never really breaks the surface—all this relieved in life by pursuits that are too good, too real, to be sacrificed by moving away: hunting, fishing, snowmobiling. And the men "talk up" the card game unflaggingly, laugh frequently, a laugh that is well-disposed and outgoing; even generous, but in fact is without mirth or gaiety—and a moment later the laughing face is settled in its accustomed tensions of holding on, determination, anger. One of the men, Ronnie, actually looks malevolent when he falls silent. He has four children, works hard in the woods buying stumpage, cutting and hauling it out—dangerous work that is insecure, subject to weather, near vanishing because of the new wood-harvesting machines. When he smiles and jokes he looks boyish, playful, and bright—then he falls silent and his face takes on the mask of a man wrongfully injured, held down or imprisoned, plotting a violent revenge. One senses an explosive rage in him, unpredictable behavior. The same, the very same description could be applied to another fellow who left the game early—also mid-thirties, a physically powerful and violent-looking man. His leaving seemed to lighten the air. The youngest, George Blodgett, has four kids, a house, a steady job at the printing company where he'll slowly rise to a certain level and no higher. The whole of his life seems to be laid out in front of him. Good friends with his father, always there, not happy in his marriage but it works, no likely changes in so small and isolated a town. He has grown rather fat and old-looking in these few years. Loves to hunt and fish, expert at both—but this stultification has overtaken him unawares; he seems to have more or less what he wants, and considers himself fortunate—which indeed, in these parts, he *is*—and he's baffled by the settled dullness of his feelings. Larry Barker works at the same print shop. At 60 he's inured to all this. But Temple was still truly rural when he was a child—there's a difference in character and outlook between the older and younger. Mert Karkis is the oldest at the table—in a way the simplest and happiest: intelligence operating in a small small purview. Follows sports on TV; less worried about the future than any of the others. Dick Blodgett on the wagon, sipping Moxie. "Well, I was drinkin' too much, enjoyin' it too much. I wanted to see if I could do without. Yeh. This not a bad drink, you want some?"

Every game is a wild one: Fiery Cross, Low Hole Roll Your Own, Queens and the Following, Midnight, Baseball—starved for liveliness and hope.

In the other room the kids are lolling on the floor watching TV. They watch it surely forty hours a week, seem stupified by it.

"Oh look at him, he's got an ace in the hole, sure he does. . . ."

"He's got Kings, back to back. . . ."

(He slacks off after betting heavily the previous round.)

"Now he's just layin' back. He's got the Kings. Well I'll bump him anyway. Oh you *do* have the Kings! Son of a gun!"

They mention the death of Joe Brackett. "The funeral's Sunday." "That'll be a well-attended funeral." "Yes, it will." No one mentions the death of Slim, which was closer to home. He had occasionally played in these games. "He came down with cancer of the stomach last September. He was just forty-nine."

Larry teases Dick about folding out of a hand when the threat turned out to be a bluff. "He's feelin' scared tonight. All you gotta do is clear your throat—he'll fold."

We play Jacks or Better, Trips to Win, the pot grows large. These are nickel and dime bets, three raises. A bad loser can be down ten to twenty dollars, which hurts many of them.

"Has the cold weather slowed you down much on that house?"

"Oh yes, there's still outside work to do."

We've been having a cold spell, ten days of it now, high winds and zero in the day. Twenty below at night. The wind keeps blowing.

"How'd you make out on your new well?"

"Good. Good. We were lucky. They hit water at 170. . . ."

"Oh that is good. Usually they go 200 around here. . . ."

"That's right. My well's 230. . . ."

"There was a well out Strong a few weeks back went damn near 500."

"They say the wells are fillin' up again. I don't see how, with all the frost in the ground and the layers of ice in the snow."

"The snow rots the ice. A lot of people don't realize that, but if you dig down through, you won't find glare ice underneath, it gets honeycombed and spongey. . . ."

"A round of Show Down? Put a dollar in. And here's for the high ace"—a separate pot—fifty cents from each.

The house is very warm, much too warm, as the custom is here; heated by the handsome old parlor stove, as good as the Jotul and better looking, a quality of cast iron you don't see anymore, from a period in which American design was superb.

The game breaks at 11:00—early. Everyone leaves quickly. Often I have stayed and talked with Dick, but tonight I'm tired.

POKER II

"Oh, he was some ball player. He played like a truck without a steering wheel. Don't you remember, Vilio, that time you were all set to catch that fly ball in the game with Strong, and Larry came charging over yelling I got it! I got it!"

"Oh God, I thought a lumber truck hit me. . . ."

"There were two men on. They all got home. Took us a while to sort out Larry and Vilio, and the ball was down in there amongst them."

"The only things was, you never knew whether he'd be drunk or sober."

"He got mad at me one day. I must of made a booboo of some kind at second base. I happened to glance up, and my god there was the ball about two feet away coming at me a hundred miles an hour. I got my glove up somehow and caught the damn thing. I carried it all the way in to Taamo and I flipped it to him. There wasn't a word spoken."

"The raccoons been at your place yet?"

"Yeah, we've had some. . . ."

"How'd that Rotenone work?"

"Well it seemed to. We haven't lost any corn since then."

"You have coons up your way?"

"Oh yes. But the dogs are pretty good with them. We usually eat a coon a year."

"You like coon?"

"It's not bad. The kids won't touch it, though. . . ."

"I've never eaten it myself. They say it's a little like chicken."

"Oh, no, it's musky, it's an oily meat. . . ."

"The coons used to devastate our corn. They'd sit in there and just knock it all down. We froze it green, just to get some. Then I happened to ask Elmer Tomlin if he was troubled by the coons—I knew damn well he wasn't 'cause his corn was just standin' there. And he said plant squash right in amongst the corn and you won't have coons. . . ."

"That's right. They won't go over it. It scratches their bellies."

" . . . It worked like a charm. I put some in the next year and we harvested all our corn. I planted squash every year. And I know it was the squash, because a couple of years ago our neighbor's kid walked all over the garden and killed the squash, and by golly the coons got in that year and took the corn."

Weikko joined the card game, fairly drunk, but, for him, happy. He had pitched the championship game which Temple had won.

"Who was in the play-off?"

"Marvin's Auto Body. We beat 'em 6–4. Goddam! Wasn't that a good game, Vilio? I may not be good for much, but I'm a good softball pitcher. God! They were biting on that drop o' mine. I get into a real crouch for that one, and I actually scrape the ground with my fingers when I throw. I don't know what it is, but they see that and it throws 'em off somehow. Wasn't that a good game, Vilio? Goddam that was a good game! I don't mean just me. I done a good job—but I mean, Smitty was great, and Bill . . . Jesus, he caught a perfect game."

Vilio: "You shoulda seen that one, George, that was a damn good game."

Weikko: "Damn right"—holds out hand to Vilio, who grins and shakes it.

POKER III

I was in a bad mood, Ronnie was ill and had to leave, George and Charlie were going smelting, Vilio wasn't there (the good humor always comes from, rests on, Vilio and Ronnie). Lindy *was* there and tends to depress things, at least for me: there's an unresolved distrust and hostility here. I don't know what it is exactly. He's a company man (a foreman at IP), and it may be that—all that that means. In any event, I felt out of place, and felt that they thought so too. There have been times when I have felt included in the warmth of their camaraderie, but tonight I felt excluded . . . and I realized how very easily that could be permanent and severe.

They belong to organizations that in a pinch would willingly put me in jail without knowing why—the American Legion, the VFW, the Knights of Columbus. And I feel that the pinch is coming.

I've been letting out diatribes of late against the draft, the corporations, the military, the nuclear industry. I let out one tonight, saying I had just learned that before the Three Mile Island accident, farmers had lost cows and chickens to low level radiation. They looked at me in silence. I didn't know whether I was spoiling the fun of the occasion or expressing an attitude which undermines them utterly, whether they agree with it or not—it takes away their livelihood, their affiliations, their competence, their ability to live in this town of their birth. The reason is that all, in effect, work for the government.

Lately Larry, Vilio, and Ronnie have been complaining angrily, as have I, about inflation, big business, etc. Tonight there was none of this. I even wondered if something special had happened—a hawkish speech at the Legion, some such.

Under pressure they'll do what they have always done, do daily, and must do in order to live here, have homes, and raise families. They'll grit their teeth, silence themselves, and do the work they have been told to do. Eventually their pain and silence will acquire a coloration of virtue and patriotism, and they'll turn on people like me, some few, viciously.

"All I've got is a small flush." (four card flush)

"You shoulda put it in. You might win."

"Well, no use startin' arguments this late at night."

POKER IV

Vilio and Toby talk about chainsaws and accidents in the woods. Dick talks about accidents cutting trees.

Vilio: "Me and Taamo . . . we was real good together with the big crosscut saw, you know. I mean . . . actually . . . we set the camp record that time in New Hampshire when we was cuttin' the blow-down pine, you know. The whole thing is . . . I mean you have to git a rhythm . . . you want to go easy and smooth, see (shows how) . . . it's like dancin' and you don't want to feel the other guy pullin' against you . . . and you don't want to push none at all . . . just easy . . . that saw goes back and forth . . . me and Taamo, we could hit a rhythm, man . . . I'm tellin' you . . . that saw just went by itself. . . . We'd be cuttin' right next to a couple of guys, you know, and they'd be sweatin' and gruntin', and puttin' their backs in it. . . . Jeez! That ain't the way. Just easy . . . easy . . . just like dancin'.'"

Toby: "The guys who invent those devices, they never worked in the woods. Rilly, those things are dangerous. What they're for is some guy's cuttin' firewood off a stack in the dooryard. You can use a brake bar then, but you can't use one in the woods, it gits in the way, like when you're limbin' a tree and you want to back-cut, or you're reachin' down in between a fork. And it's the same with ear plugs, they're dangerous. You've gotta be able to hear a twig snappin'. I'd be dead right now if I wore those christly things. It's happened to me a number o' times. I'll hear the snapping, and Christ Almighty, a tree I hit the day before when I felled the other one has finally broke off and is comin' down. If I had those damned ear plugs on I'd never hear it. Drive me right in the ground. Nobody wears those damn things in the woods. And now one of the worst things of all is these damn safety boots they've come up with. I mean the winter pacs, not regular steel toe boots. They're about this long. They stick way the hell out beyond your toes. Jesus! You're stumblin' all over the place and trippin' on limbs. I hate the goddam things. And if there's an emergency and you want to move fast, why . . . you move your natural way . . . I mean you know where your feet end, and what you're moving is your feet. They're dangerous. But you gotta wear 'em now if you're workin' for one o' the big companies."

Vilio: "It's gettin' so . . . Jesus . . . I'd as soon stay home and take food stamps. There's so many regulations and laws, and they ain't to the advantage of the ones that really does the work. It's like Toby says . . . the guys that dreamed these things up, you know . . . *they* never worked in the woods."

One of the wonderful things about Dick, Vilio, Ronnie, Toby (not George and Charlie so much, and not Lindy at all, who is self-centered and smug) is the powerful good feeling that rises up among them, the strong affection for one another. This is especially true of Vilio, and especially when he's got a slight buzz on. As the night (poker in progress) wears on, he smiles that wonderful open-hearted smile more and more frequently, and begins to pay compliments and shake hands . . . and you see that what he really wants to do is *hold* hands; these are embraces.

Vilio (after a long talk about the Selectman's duties and how he plans to retire next year): "I'll tell you one thing. There's nobody I appreciate more than that guy sittin' right there. I mean it. Put 'er there, Dick." (Reaches his hand across the table.)

Dick (grinning, taking Vilio's hand): "Here we go again."

Vilio (holding): "Him and me have known each other since we was boys. When he was growin' up he was like he is now. He has always been the straightest, squarest guy. . . ."

Toby: "It's true. He is the most honored man around here. It really is, Dick."

Dick: "Good second baseman, anyway."

(Vilio grins and lets go of his hand.)

Vilio: "Yes, you was a good second baseman. (grins) Maybe you needed a little help from the infield now and then."

Dick: "And they could give it too, when they were awake. They were a smart bunch."

Vilio (laughs, then soberly): "We was a damn good ball club. It's really surprisin' when you think how old we were when we really started playin'. I mean playin' regular like that. I was twenty-eight years old. So was Taamo, and God, with that arm o' his . . . he could've been playin' in the majors. (to me) You'd have to see it to believe it. He was *good*. Dick, you remember that time we played the farm team from Boston?"

Dick: "Oh yeah. Oh sure. They thought they'd have an easy time. What'd they give us that night? Fifty dollars? They just needed opponents, see. It was an exhibition game right here in Farmington at the Fair Grounds."

Vilio: "We beat 'em, by God! They was the most surprised bunch o' guys."

Dick: "Taamo beat 'em."

Vilio: "That's right. Taamo struck out twelve men that night. Jesus! That man had an arm."

Dick: " 'Course second base backed him up pretty strong."

Vilio: "Did you get a hit that night?"

Dick: "What do you mean *a* hit? I got my usual four hits."

Vilio: "Once in the stomach, once in the head . . . There must o' been somethin' about the way you looked that threw that pitcher off. . . ."

Dick: "He was scared."

Vilio: "That's what I mean. Ha! ha! Put 'er there, Dick. No, I'll tell you. You was a damn good ball player. (to me) Everything this guy ever did, he did it just right, by God."

Dick: "That last hand was pretty good, wasn't it."

Vilio: "What's that?"

Dick: "I said I dealt that last hand pretty good. You had three kings, didn't you?"

Vilio: "Oh yeah, that was good dealin'. That's what I mean."

Dick: "Wasn't what I *meant* to do. I meant to put 'em over *here*. But just so they was goin' *some*where."

Vilio: "Well, now that you got the hang of it, you stick right with it."

Dick: "Well, we'll see. I'm still learnin'."

Toby (who'd been losing): "You're doin' all right, aren't you?"

Dick: "Oh, a couple dollars maybe."

A few minutes later, when Vilio was shuffling the cards, his hands, that were essentially fine-boned, shapely hands, of a good size though not large, but now were distorted by accidents and arthritis and also by the lifelong pressure of chainsaw handles, so that the pads of his thumbs were very large, the joints of many fingers swollen, the left wrist misshapen where it had been caught by a falling tree and broken (his neck, too, had been broken by a falling tree; his two boys had saved his life)—when he was shuffling the cards, they slipped out of his fingers several times, and he had trouble picking them up. "God-damn!" he said, "My hands are gittin' so *goddam old!*"

Later he said he was going to retire next year as selectman, and added, "I'm not sure I'll even be around next year."

"Oh yeah," Dick said, "all you need's a good toupee, you'd be good for another twenty years."

During a halt in the game, while Toby went to the bathroom, Dick said gravely that Helen would have to be operated on again in three weeks. He said, "That last operation was forty-five minutes. This one's scheduled for three hours."

Vilio: "Did you get the lab report?"

Dick: "Yeah, that's all been done. She's got problems."

Vilio: "Well Dick, lemme tell you . . . it helps to pray. It's the one thing that in all cases really helps."

Dick: "Oh, sure . . . sure. Doctor Smith will be doing it. He's good, he's real good. We've both got faith in him."

Vilio: "Just so she keeps her courage. An' knowin' Helen, I know she will."

Dick: "She's got lots o' courage. She'll come through."

Toby came back, and noticed the tone, and questioned Dick, who said, "It's Helen. She'll be goin' to the hospital in three weeks. Yeh. She needs an operation. She's got problems. But we've got a good man doin' it. We'll come through."

Toby saw that this was something Dick didn't want to pursue further. Since nothing could be gained by gloominess, the talkative good spirits soon came back.

Vilio again mentioned retirement. Dick said, "Oh, you'll be selectman for quite a while yet. You've been selectman longer than anybody in the history of this town."

Vilio: "Rilly?"

Dick: "Oh yes. Oh I'm sure o' that. You been selectman twenty-five years now. Dad was selectman—and he was road commissioner. I was selectman eleven years."

Vilio: "You and me started together. That was my first year, and it was yours, too."

Dick: "That's right. So that makes it twenty-two years."

Vilio: "That's right."

Dick: "If you ain't wrecked the town by now, you prob'ly can't do it, so you might's well stay on."

Toby: "Maybe one more year is all he needs. You better watch out."

Vilio: "Seriously, don't you think it's time I got the hell out o' there?"

Dick: "No."

Vilio: "You mean I got to stay on?"

Dick: "Yeh."

Vilio: "Deal the goddam cards." (everyone laughs)

Toby: "Both you guys ought to quit workin' an' just devote yourself to huntin' and fishin'."

Dick: "Well I don't know. I like to go out still. I went out a couple times this year with George and the boys, but I really don't want to shoot nothin' anymore. I don't know. I just don't."

Toby: "Oh, I love to hunt."

Dick: "So does George. And I still go out, you know. But I don't have the same feeling for it. Now Rick's comin' along just like George. He's good at it, too. He notices everything. Not just in the woods, either—everywhere. He's just as sharp as can be. I can go into a house and not see a damn thing. I couldn't tell you what color the carpet was or whether they had wallpaper or painted walls—but Rick sees everything. He's like that on the snowmobile, too. He sees what's in front and what's in back and what's on both sides. I like that."

Toby: "He's got George's sharp eye, too."

Dick: "George is a good shot."

Toby: "Oh, I guess. . . ."

Dick: "You know I had that little trout pond up here for the boys. That little beaver pond right up back. I put two hundred fish in it one year, and another hundred the next, and we was doin' fine, then an otter come along and cleaned us right out. So George sat up in the field across the road, by the shack there, and that otter come along, quite early. Well you know that's a good two hundred yards, and George put that bullet right through its head. One shot. Right through the head. And I remember once there was a woodchuck down at Gorder's eatin' up the garden, and George got out behind the old parsonage there just before it got light. Now that's a good three hundred yards. And he put the bullet right through its head. And that's with open sights."

Vilio: "I'll take open sights any day."

Toby: "Well I will too in the woods. But for an open shot you can't beat a scope. Mine I can use either way. The scope sets up high—I can sight beneath it if I want to, or I can use the scope. You know I never can figure out how that scope works. If it sets up high like, you'd think the line o' the bullet and the line o' the scope would converge at some point, and anything beyond that point they'd pass right by each other. . . ."

Dick talked about cutting some fine large pine years ago, with an old Stihl chainsaw. "It had plenty of power but it was slow. You could see the teeth on it." (Five horsepower. "Our saws today are five horse-power but they're high speed.")

Accidents again. I asked what made the saws jump back, and why some were more dangerous than others. Vilio and Toby talked at the same time. I didn't like to choose between father and son. Toby said to Vilio, "Go ahead, Dad." And Vilio said, "Go ahead"—but Vilio talked. He said, "If the tip o' the saw hits something, it'll climb right up, it'll jump right up . . . A strong man can't hold it."

Toby: "That's why so many accidents happen with guys cuttin' their own wood in the dooryard."

Vilio: "That's right. It's the most dangerous place of all."

Toby: "They're cuttin off the pile, and the tip o' the saw is always hittin' the next log. With a high speed saw like the Partner, you can't hold it. And your hands is too close together anyway. All three times I've been cut it's been with the Partner. The only thing that saved my face—and maybe it saved my life, rilly—I got my hand up to my face before the saw." (Shows cuts.)

Vilio: "They ain't cuts, really, they're *tears*. I'll tell you, boy, a chain-saw cut . . . (he shakes his head) . . . it ain't like a knife cut . . . it's a mean thing. . . ."

Toby: "I've been doin' well with the Husqvarna. The grip is fur-ther apart and for some reason it just don't jump up the way the Partner does."

Vilio: "The Homelite's a safe saw to use, but you can't get no work out of it. And they just don't hold up. I'd rather use American-made products, but what the hell . . . I mean, we gotta eat. We gotta go with the best product. We like the Husqvarna. It's a damn good saw."

I: "What can you do to keep the saw from jumping up?"

Vilio: "Well, you have to know what you're doin'. The main thing is, keep the end o' the saw projectin' a few inches beyond the stick you're cuttin'. But you gotta keep your eyes open, especially when you're tired."

Toby: "Like Monday morning. . . ."

Vilio (laughs): "Yeah, it don't help bein' hung over. And when the light is bad. . . ."

Toby: "Did you hear what happened to Bunnel? He was workin' alone, way back in. He had to walk more'n a mile. I guess he was fellin' firewood, you know, and let it sit with the leaves on, then make the road and skid it out in the fall. Well, I don't know exactly how it happened, but a tree come down right across him and broke both legs. He had to drag himself more'n a mile to the car. He'd go a while then stop and smoke his pipe, then go some more. Boy, I'll tell you . . . I don't know how he got up in that cab. I don't know how he worked the brakes and the clutch. Drove himself all the way to the hospital. . . ."

Charlie: "God!"

Toby: "He's a good cutter, too."

Dick: "That's a hard luck family. The whole family had to have them rabies shots a couple years back—the ones they stick in your belly. . . ."

Vilio: "It happens to the best cutters same as it happens to the worst. Maybe not as much."

Toby: "Not nearly as much. Don't forget, you're talking about an ungodly number of hours under all conditions."

Vilio: "All conditions except good ones."

Toby: "Right."

Vilio: "Jesus, every time I see Buster Hazlitt . . . I don't know . . . it makes me sick what has happened to that poor guy. And he wasn't just *good*. He was *tops*. Am I right, Toby? He was *tops!*"

Toby: "Oh God yes! That guy was a phenomenon. Me and Pop and Weikko, we're good cutters, we're damn good workmen. There ain't many guys can keep up with us. But *Buster!* We couldn't keep up with him. I never saw a guy move so smooth and quick. Not a wasted step. He could size up a stand o' trees so when he'd limbed one he'd be right at the next one he wanted to fell. He'd go up and down a stand like that. God it was sump'in to see! Cheerful, crackin' jokes all the time! That man could heave cordwood off a truck as fast as a cherry picker. Damn near, anyway. And he wasn't big. He was plenty rugged, but he wasn't big. It was just the way he moved. He had wonderful balance. And he'd stay real close to the wood. You have to. But not many guys can really do it. I watched him unload some rock maple one day. That's eighty or a hundred, a hundred-twenty pounds to a stick, and Jesus, he'd flip those sticks outa the truck and you'd see the pile grow up right there alongside, so neat nobody ever had to stack it again. And he'd be talkin' and crackin' jokes all the time."

Vilio: "He was workin' by himself one Saturday up the side of Spruce Mountain, 'bout four miles from the tarred road, and he slipped, or God knows what, 'n he cut his whole foot and ankle right off, right clean through the bone, the whole goddam way. I don't know how the hell he got outa there, but he did. He got all the way out and got as far as Ed Tolliver's place, and thank God Ed was home. Jesus!"

Toby: "I see him in Samm's now and then on crutches. His face looks like he cries all night instead of sleepin'. Buddy says he drinks a fifth a day, and a couple of six packs on top of it. He used to weigh about a hundred-sixty, he's around two-forty now."

Vilio: "Maybe he'll pull out of it."

Toby: "He's got to. He'll be dead if he don't."

Vilio: "That's right. If he could just get his mind *set* the right way. He ain't finished, but he *thinks* he is. He could get one o' these artificial limbs and prob'ly go back to work."

Toby: "They're expensive as hell."

Vilio: "So's a bottle a day! God! That stuff ain't cheap."

Toby: "You got a point there. They make amazin' artificial limbs now. You can flex 'em and everything."

Vilio: "Old Ken Hoar's been cuttin' quite a few years now on that damn wooden leg, and that damn thing starts up near the hip. . . ."

Toby: "He don't cut no seven eight nine ten cord a day, neither. And there ain't nobody gonna hire 'im."

Vilio: "He works for himself. But at least he makes a go of it."

Toby: "He's a nice old guy, don't get me wrong. He ain't no Buster Hazlitt, that's all. Buster was top man. There was none better, not a single one."

Vilio: "That's right."

Dick said, "I heard you had a little trouble with your skidder."

Toby: "Oh, I guess."

I: "What happened?"

Toby: "Me and Weikko was cuttin' up on Deam Mountain right close to the ledges, and I was movin' the skidder right along there where the ledges pitch down, it's all rock, you know, there ain't a spoonful o' dirt on it . . . it gits a bit slick. Well I knew I was bein' stupid, but when you're stupid you're stupid, there's prob'ly no help for it. I was savin' all of five minutes, I'm sure. So naturally, the exact place I was worried about pitched me over. The damn skidder slid sideways right down the ledge . . . and then it came to a stop on an angle like this. Jeeezuz. I didn't know *what* to do. I didn't know what was holdin' me. I didn't dare turn the wheels, or move them. Gawd! I'z afraid if I blinked or coughed we'd go right over . . . We've got forty thousand in that damn machine. . . ."

Vilio: "Plus ten or twelve dollars in the driver."

Toby: "He ain't worth that much. Not from the neck up, anyway. I was even afraid to shout for Weikko. I didn't know *what* was holdin' me, some little peg o' rock. But Weikko saw what had happened and he come runnin' . . . So I passed him the cable an' he run up with it and carried it around a good sized tree and came back with it and hitched it on front . . . and we winched her right up slicker'n hell. But I'll tell you, when we had that thing on solid ground again, I didn't feel like doin' nuthin' for five or six minutes. Weikko neither. We just sat there nice and quiet and drank a couple o' beers."

Charlie: "Well Toby, you always do take that skidder into places nobody else would go."

Toby: "I've had good luck so far. I mean, I've had a few close ones. . . ."

Vilio: "A few hundred. . . . " (laughs)

Toby: "Well . . . maybe I've learned my lesson."

Dick talked about the early days of his tenure as selectman. He said what a strange bunch the Gallups were.

Dick: "Kenneth Gallup come around and said he wanted to be chief o' police o' the town of Temple. He wanted to put it on the warrant for the town meeting. Well, I wouldn't sign it. 'Twere a foolish notion. What's a little town like this need a police chief for? A constable, all right. So I said to him, Kenneth, if you'd like to be constable you can start right in this Saturday night keeping the peace at the dance hall. Ha ha! That changed his mind right quick. He said, oh no, no thanks."

Charlie: "You had a lot o' fights there."

Dick: "Well I guess . . . yeah. Vilio and I used to take turns keepin' things peaceful, but it wasn't always easy."

Vilio: "The trouble was . . . once you got the warring parties outside and made peace among 'em, then you had to have a drink with 'em . . . There's many a night I woulda been better off if I had let them fight. God! I drank some awful stuff in those days."

Dick: "Everybody did. That was the most popular brand."

Dick's story of conflict with the Gallups: Gallup senior brought his big son in with him, and the son was wearing gloves (warm weather) and was ready to fight.

Dick: "I came awful close to givin' that guy a punch in the nose . . . and I was well able to in those days."

Vilio: "There was very few guys willin' to find out."

Vilio mentioned that Mr. Hutchins had sold his land to Bob Bull, who therefore now abuts me. I asked Vilio if he knew the price.

Vilio: "No, I don't. I mean I *do* know what was paid for it, but I can't divulge it. It wouldn't be right. See, the reason I know is because

I'm selectman and it would be unethical if I went around talkin' about it. It was a good price, that's all I can say."

Early, regarding George Blodgett's absence.
Dick: "He said he wasn't feelin' well."
Toby: "He prob'ly ought to go to the hospital if he felt bad enough to miss poker."

Dick: "Years ago we lived where George Andrews lives now, and I could look out the window in the afternoon and see the teams lined up on the other side o' the hill there. I was just a little shaver then. Later we moved to the house the Lynches have now. The teams would come in from Mount Blue. They had lumber camps up there. Five cords o' birch on a wagon, two hosses. 'Course they'd all try t'get more on than the next man. They'd be lined up on the Intervale, takin' turns goin' up the hill by Andrews. It was higher then, much higher; it's been levelled off. They had to give the hosses a rest, let them get their wind, or they couldn't make that hill, then they'd go on down the other side and try to keep up speed, and swerve where the log pile was, hopin' the load would tip over, see, so they wouldn't have to unload it. See, the mill was downhill from where the new store is now."

Just a few days after the conversation about chainsaw injuries, I saw Vilio at the store. There was an uncharacteristic stubble of beard on his face, and a strange discoloration and distortion at the corner of his mouth. When I came closer, I saw that there was a large L-shaped cut at the corner of his mouth. I said, "Vilio, did you get hurt?"

He said, "Yeah, the saw caught me. It's comin' along good, though. Don't pain me none. But they better take the stitches out soon so I can shave."

I saw Toby Helgren outside and asked how it had happened. He said, "Saw jumped up, that's all. They put fifty stitches in 'im. The cut went all the way inside, too. He was lucky. A few inches up, it could've taken out his eye. A few inches down it could've caught 'im in the throat and prob'ly killed 'im."

"You ought to get him out of the woods."

"We're tryin' to."

"I know you are."

"He'll be sixty-five next October. We'd like for him to quit, or just do enough to keep active, you know."

"At the age he's at it's too easy to get tired, and then the accidents happen."

"Yeah, but this happened first thing in the morning."

"You're in a rough line of work. The insurance companies say it's the most dangerous in the world."

"Don't I *know* that! We pay thirty-four dollars on the hundred for workman's comp. Can you imagine that? Thirty-four dollars out of every hundred goes to the insurance companies. You have to work twice as hard to make ends meet, and the harder you work the more you cut yourself up. Partly it's because we don't have no organization to represent us. No union. But you can't have one. You can't organize woodcutters. They got us over a barrel. We gotta meet payments on the machines or we lose everything. Same as the comp. You can't git no ticket without it."

Maynard's Fingers

Maynard: "Look at that." (Holds out his finger; strange, blunt tip. It's trembling.) "There's no tip there. I mean it's just a hunk o' meat, there's no blood vessels or nothin'. It gets *colder'n* hell. And it's better if I work with my gloves off, there's no circulation down there. A gas tank popped it off, squeezed it right off just the way you'd squeeze a pimple. It was down at Harry Blodgett's old place. Harry was still alive then. I was movin' one of those tanks an' it slipped off the truck and came right at me. That's what it caught, I moved everything else. I knew what'd happened. I didn't have to look. I was wearin' gloves. I finished hookin' it up and loaded the truck and drove off. I thought I could drive into Farmington hospital all right, but then before I got to

Slim's store I made the mistake of taking off my glove. Oh, didn't she spurt! The tip was hangin' on there by a piece o' skin, an' the bone was showin'. Every time I shifted gears there was a new streak of blood on the window or the dashboard. I went into Slim's store and shouted 'Slim! Can you drive me to Farmington?' He was sittin' in back workin' on his books. He said, 'Sure, when you want to go?' I said, 'Right now.' He looked over at me and said, 'Jesus Christ, let's go!' I said, 'Don't you want to close up the store?' That fat old Finn was in it . . . who was that now? I can't think of his name. Do you know who I mean? Well, he was a Finn. Slim said no, this fellow would look after it. The safe was wide open and everything. He wasn't worried. When we got t' the hospital the doctor said, 'What do you want me to do with it? Cut it off?' I said, 'Hell no, sew it on! If that don't work we can cut it off later.' He said, 'You want me to freeze it?' I said, 'Don't freeze nothin'. I'll hold it in place and you sew it.' So he stitched it right up. Next day was when I felt it. I kept my hand right up in the air like a smart little boy at school. It felt a whole lot better that way."

He moulded a sharp point on another finger. "There's nothin' on this one but a piece o' meat. See what you can do when it gets cold? You can bring it right to a point just like a piece o' putty. I cut this one off with an axe when I was a kid."

I asked him if he went out much in the evening.

"Not often. When I get home I'm usually tired. An' then I do a lot o' the cookin'. Oh yeah, I bake all the bread, pies, rolls. We don't buy that stuff at the store. Oh, it's rotten. I baked eighty doughnuts last Saturday—fifty regular and thirty chocolate. I'm going to bake some apple pie tonight. I have my apples all cut and frozen. Same with the squash. If I don't have anything to do in the evening, I'll sit there and slice apples.

"We love to dance. At the last Charity Ball we came in number two in the waltz and number two in the jitterbug. We should've won the waltz outright, but they gave it to some old bastard who was seventy-five or eighty. They weren't waltzin'. She was just going in reverse an' he was going straight ahead. Hazel and I are pretty good. I'm a hard man to dance with 'cause I put in a lot o' steps o' my own, but she and I been dancin' together for twenty-five years now and she knows what I'm going to do even before I do."

JIM FLAGG'S BACK

"I had back trouble wicked bad, my lower back, you know. I went to every doctor around, I had x-rays. It got so bad I'd just drive around and if I saw a doctor's office I'd go in. Nobody helped at all. So I said to myself, goddam, I ain't gonna spend my life a cripple. . . . Now you may not believe what happened, but it happened, so help me God. I figured, I hurt it workin', I'll cure it workin'. I had a four-foot stick o' pine out back, musta been two feet across. I went out and took one end of it and lifted. I did it right, I bent my knees, I used my whole body, and my back hurt like hell, but I said, you son of a bitch, either kill me or clear out. I lifted it several times. And I did my old army exercises, you know, twisting and touching your toes and all that. I went out every day and lifted that pine and did those exercises. After about a week the pain changed . . . it still hurt, but it was a sweet pain, if you know what I'm talkin' about . . . and then a couple weeks more and it didn't hurt at all. That was ten years ago. I ain't been troubled since then, not even a little."

He owned the secondhand store in Farmington Falls.

"At that time, back in the early sixties, the wood prices kept falling. It cost you eight dollars to make ten. I saw it was gonna get worse, so I got out. I bought that business from Hinckley. I could see he wasn't tending to it—he was never there when you called—so I figured probably a small demand had built up. I bought the business for $600—not a good deal, probably, but not real bad, either. And I made out all right with it. My wife did the selling and I did the hauling. When she died I lost interest in everything. But I had to raise the kids. . . . Everybody was hurtin' then, real bad a lot o' them . . . that was that recession. . . . I thought maybe I could get that business goin' again . . . but people started the yard sales and that ruined it . . . nobody'd buy my junk when they could get a better price right down the street and maybe sell their own junk at the same time.

"I remember Dutchy Larned. I bought some of that stuff when he died. Well, that store o' mine was a big building, too. It was like a maze, you couldn't find the end of it. I just used a small part of it."

Working with Jim, with the woodsplitter:

"It's got all kind 'o power, but it's not engineered very well. I had t' make several changes. The blade was slanted back instead o' forward, and the blade was too small—I welded that other blade on top, and you can see the seam down there where I took the whole head off and changed the angle."

We were handling some huge pieces. I said, "This one's extra heavy," meaning, *should I help?* Jim is strong and skillful and in general lets you know that a certain kind of help is a hindrance. All I did was keep pieces laid out at his feet so he could lift them onto the splitter. When I said, "This one's extra heavy," and stood by to help, he grinned and said, "I'll use extra strength."

Uses knees, hips, etc. to heave the big ones up. They weigh 120, 130, 140. Maybe a third of the wood was like that.

"It's really harder cutting it on the pile—you know you have to lift in really bad positions. But I'd rather cut than split. I just got this splitter to do my own wood and a few people. I'll get it paid off this year, then I'll just do a few jobs with it."

POKER AT RONNIE'S CAMP

At Ronnie's camp on Porter Lake in late June.

Ronnie's sons, Lindy's sons, George's sons all fishing and running back and forth. (These fathers do a lot with their sons, sports, Little League, hunting, guns, fishing. The boys are really brought up in the local competences.)

Clans. Visiting friends, several wives talk while we play (we are on the closed porch, they in the small living room).

Talk of the new hunting-camp/guide service they're opening.

The sweetness of twilight on the lake.

They pay a heavy price all week long, belonging to their employers, working very very hard. But their relations among themselves are in many ways wonderful—honorable, self-respecting and respecting of each other. Courteous, helpful, extremely competent. Challenging and meeting peer challenge in competing and the ongoing prime virtue of courage. They don't complain. Ronnie says, "I come home bone tired, just bone tired"—but it's not a complaint, very objective, factual: hard cutting, bad weather, low prices at the mills. Vilio cuts his face, breaks neck, etc., never complains. They are extremely conservative and are ignorant of the larger world both willfully and simply because there is no time or means. The willful aspect means *don't rock the boat*.

POKER AT CASEY'S CAMP

Fishing trip to Moosehead Lake (in Spencer Bay, at Casey's Camps).

Casey's coyotes—fourteen skinned, on ground (woodchips, some ashes, dirty snow). Looking like grayhounds, a couple of inches cut from the forward lower jaw, so that state biologists could study their teeth, which give clues to growth. Three unskinned, hanging head down from rafter of the front porch, very large, like wolves, a *surprising* size. Two litters a year, up to eight pups.

Most of these were snared in steel wire snares (special permit required; in this he works for the state). Two or three had been shot. He had the remains of a coyote deer-kill in the back of his truck. Probably uses that for bait. He showed us a twisted steel cable, ruined. "Don't they jump around!"

Casey—small, strong, *ready,* almost combative, a cunning look, a look almost paranoiac in its sharpness and readiness to see affront or exploitation. Laconic. ("You wouldn't want him for an enemy." "I'd like to have 'im on my side, that's for sure.") Yet when treated well, he becomes informative and friendly. Speaks with great seriousness and judiciousness, an expert at what he does, and he shows the set-apart quality and the pride of an expert. Good-looking young wife, rugged (picked up tail-end of snowmobile, moved it with a single, decisive heave). She, to Casey, who held a camera, "Why don't you shoot this nice cusk I caught, and forget about them ugly coyotes!" (A twelve and a half pound cusk, caught through the ice the night before.)

Our large log cabin, right on the water—excellent taxidermy—five or six deer (moose, fisher, mink, fox and albino fox, horns and antlers).

Ronnie's nine-year-old son, sweet and tender and shy, but he holds his shoulders as his daddy does, and walks like a man ready to put his back to something heavy and ready to ignore the scraping of the hands and the minor cuts involved in all the work up here. His bearing says, "I don't pity myself. I don't turn away just because it hurts."

Ronnie: "How do you peel garlic?" (I say: "Smash it.")

Casey: "Well, in a kitchen you usually have a pot of deep fat going, so you just cut the tips off the cloves and toss 'em in the fat, just about a minute, not more. Then you can rub a whole handful between your hands and the skin'll come right off. There's a trick like that with grapefruit, too, if you're going to section 'em. Put 'em in boiling water for about thirty seconds. They'll come right apart. In a restaurant I use a dishwasher for that. Just put it on the rinse cycle and throw in the grapefruit."

He worked as cook, cook-manager, etc., in restaurants for fifteen years.

Vilio drank so much beer he kept forgetting what game we were playing. But enjoyed it all immensely, laughing and shaking hands across the table, as he does, and patting shoulders. (He sits beside Dick regularly at Friday poker (and George Blodgett on the other side of Dick), and often Vilio will clap Dick on the shoulder and say, "By God, him and me have known each other . . . (he seems to go blank, then he grins and says) at least a hundred years, wouldn't you say, Dick?" Dick calls him Helgren—an old rural manner Dick connects with farming traditions, Vilio with the woods.

"Gettin' kinda stemmy."

[JOURNAL]

FEBRUARY 28

A bad winter—early snow, but then lots of rain, overcast skies, ice, followed by a twenty day cold snap with −20 degree nights and an unremitting high wind. At the end of all this the snow was like a densely packed honeycomb and was so hard that the ponies could run where they wanted to. I happened to be watching them from the upper window when they made the discovery that the snow would hold them. They kicked up their heels again and again and galloped up and down the slopes by the house, or rather across them in looping arcs. Prior to this they had been confined to their be-shat brown paths near the barn, and the ploughed road. They've been nibbling young beeches at the edge of the woods.

I've gone into the woods out back only four times this winter. After the three weeks of wind the snow in the woods was incredibly dirty— bark, dead branches, clumps of pine needles, birch bark strewn everywhere and actually gathered in depth in old tracks, both of animals and skis. There were many blow-downs, especially tall spruce, whose full tops caught the wind.

One virtue of this kind of snow is that I can go everywhere on the skis and it's no work at all, whereas if I'm breaking trail in deep snow, bushwhacking becomes tiring. I went along the inlet down to Drury Pond (Woody running beside me), the length of it to the beaver dam on the outlet, then back and through the woods to the pickerel pond, where there were a dozen ice-fishing holes not yet iced up; then through the woods to the Owen Mann place (the barns are down utterly) and home. That was a couple of weeks ago.

Today was warm and brilliantly sunny (little sun all winter)—I had to squint and thought for a moment I ought to go get my sunglasses. The trunks of the birches were a dazzling white. Even the poplars were bright. Once in the woods my eyes stopped smarting. Black shadows of trees everywhere against the brilliant snow. There had been enough of a snowfall to cover the debris, and the forest floor was white again. It had been a wet, heavy, typical spring snow—then a freeze last night, making a breakable crust. No animal tracks in the short distance I went. Birch bark flapping on the trunks, torn up by the wind but not blown off. Birches well-budded, their fine upper branches looking feathery against the sky; poplar buds fat, beech buds well along. Woody and Sashka ran with me, breaking through the crust and working mightily.

MARCH 16

I drove to Reeds, put on the skis there and went along the Orbeton Stream on the old railroad bed of the Sandy River-Rangeley line. This is a snowmobile highway to Reddington Pond and the tracks were terribly icy. A sunny, brisk day, without much wind.

I don't know whether the Orbeton froze solid this winter or not, but it has obviously been flowing for several weeks, a slate black flow between ice banks and under ice sheets and between snow-capped boulders and around snowy sand bars.

The Orbeton is a large stream, shallow, incredibly rocky, fast, noisy. Pebbles, rocks, boulders, passages that seem to be gouged and carved out of outcroppings of ledge, but are probably simply the carved tops of gigantic boulders. Snow and ice are everywhere except where the water has cut through. There are places of deep, translucent buildup of frozen spray. The banks are vertical, layered walls of snow. Here and there a long trunk of some uprooted tree is wedged into the wall at a slight angle. The ice extends away from the banks. Part of the stream on both sides is ice, only a turbulent channel in the middle is flowing.

Alders, mixed evergreens, birches, maples—the stream-side trees seem battered, just standing there enduring things—very different, this, from their appearance in summer, fortified by green, triumphant in green. And the green joins them one to another, so that they seem to be a host, a *place,* and the stream then is a mere (though beautiful) presence in that place. But now the trees are like the lonely crowds of the cities, standing there in their multitudes, each one alone.

So many different colors in the ice, which has piled up, been built up by different means: accumulated spray, freezing films—and over so many surfaces of sand and rock. There are places where the ice is almost yellow (accumulated spray by a small waterfall—and already the trout pool below it stirs me) and places where it is almost green—all this set off by the brilliant white of the snow on all the rocks, bars, and bridges of ice. There are still sheets of ice going straight across, and the water flows beneath them. The sheets range in color from a silvery gray to a dark, brownish gray where the water is showing through. Alders, growing on the snow-covered sandbars, thrust up their curved, barren stalks. The whole scene—so much black and white, so many sepias and cold browns—reminds me continually of drawings I've seen, and of Bruegel and Holbein, the latter not for any landscapes but for the colors of some small drawings, portraits, I saw once at the Morgan—cold colors, like these.

I went beyond the Reddington line, to within a mile of Reddington Pond. The air was cooling, the sun getting low, and I was exhausted—time to turn back. The deer can move around on this hardened snow, there were tracks, and (once) the tracks of a moose—also raccoon, fox, partridge (and I saw two that seemed like powerful year-olds) and snowshoe hare.

Exciting place where the valley of the Orbeton broadens immensely and is deep and far from the trail, with the huge ridge beyond it, and snowy, blue-black mountains in the distance.

I kept looking for stump-dried black spruce to take for canoe poles, and saw two, finally, side by side. But I was too tired to take them—too far to go.

The trail was so icy that in spite of the gentleness of the grade I was able to go back just by poling. But this was exhausting finally—it would have been better if I had been able to stride.

Walked over the Persham Bridge, a little rickety, but the snow-mobiles go over it.

There was more snow here than in Temple. Portland was almost free of snow. And in Boston it was nearly spring.

Here at home the hilly stretches of the road that face west have already thawed, been rutted, and frozen again. The hill that tilts toward the sun thaws much ahead of the flat similarly oriented. There are a few places on the hill below the house where the earth is showing through.

MARCH 23

Bright, hot sun, two days in a row. The ponies were lying on the road at the top of hill, maximum sun. Rolled up awkwardly.

Wasps, the black, long, wiry ones, going this way and that on the woodshed door at the house, exploring.

The dooryard, where it was plowed, is wholly bare—muddy, soupy brown grass, showing the ponies' hooves, the dogs' feet, our boots. Deep ruts in the road, watery everywhere, some puddles, some collapsing. The road could easily collapse this year, down below. A couple of the old corduroy logs pushing up, as usual.

From Portland to Waterville the fields are entirely brown. Here there are still many fields with snow. But there are brown patches. Varying thicknesses of snow—from nothing to a couple of feet. In the woods you can still walk on top of it, except that you break through every other step. The snow is granular, composed almost entirely of ice particles. The streams are flowing fast. Temple Stream is like a river, high and powerful. There's still ice across Drury Pond, gray ice.

The sun has taken the snow down remarkably in two days. Someone told of thrusting a shovel into the snow in the morning, and the snow held it erect. That evening the shovel was lying on bare ground.

Many flies buzzing indoors on the sunny windows.

I stopped at Mr. Fife's to talk a while, and he said, "Look! Is that a bee! Yes, by gurry, it's a bee! The first one! I'll have to write that down."

One of the Pug dogs down at the Harrises' is in heat. Shem and Woody have been down there for three days.

I went a short way into the woods at noon. The glare of sun on snow was blinding. Even the birches were almost painfully bright.

The buds on the trees are all fatter. The apple buds are covered with a pale, milky velvet. The small side shoots have a sheen of the same.

All the trees in the fields have wide rings of bare ground (grass, leaves, weeds, little saplings) around them. Those in the woods, too, but the rings are much smaller.

Across some of the fields in the Intervale there are beginning to be visible the usual raised tracks of skis, the packed snow melting more slowly than the rest. Later the snowmobile tracks will look the same—but they are deeper to begin with; the melting must go on a while.

Sap buckets have been hanging from the roadside maples for several days. Sap-boiling rigs in front of some of the houses, e.g. Kimbers. A large, flat evaporating tray is sectioned in along the top of a fifty-gallon drum that serves as a stove, propped on legs, lengthwise. A stovepipe sticks up three or four feet at the end. A good rig. They have two of these.

MARCH 24

Warm again. Road softer, deeply rutted now. We may have to confine our driving to early morning and late at night, while the mush is frozen, or at least firmer.

But late in the afternoon massive gray clouds came in from the west—bright sky showing through here and there, blue sky and white clouds in the east—but then the gray took over and late in the evening it began to rain. Rained on and off all night, never heavily, but enough to increase the run-off hugely. The roaring of water was louder here on the hill.

I was afraid the softening mud of the road would soon be impassable. Mabel's VW wouldn't start. I took the Saab down. Surprised by floodwaters at the bottom. Left the car at Eddie's and chatted with him. Went to look at Drury Pond, thinking that if I could walk across it would save me almost a mile. The ice is still thick in the center, but there are cracks in it, lots of water on top here and there; by the shore the ice was sunken, the top water a foot deep in a few places. I probed the closest ice with a stick and it went right through—a foot and a half of mush.

I walked back the usual way, going out into the main road to check for flooding. The new drainage ditch was two thirds filled with turbid, heavily racing water. The culvert under the road—from Lynch's field to Rosie Blodgett's was pouring a strong stream into the water of the ditch, but there were sheets of water in the lower end of Lynch's swampy field, and on the other side I could see that the farther, lower section of Rosie's was flooded. A thin sheet of water poured across the road from Lynch's field to Rosie's.

I remembered seeing trout in that drainage ditch last year.

A fine, misty rain, pleasant to be in. Cecil and Kevin, who had spent so much time helping me lure Woody home, using the little Pug in heat as bait, saw me and accompanied me as far as the wooden bridge, coats open and hats on the back of their heads. Kevin didn't have boots and so walked on the snowbanks. Cecil waded through the flooded hollows of the road, as did I. The water was a foot deep.

Cecil said, "Jeee-zum! Lookit the stream! It's as high as the road. It's a good thing these snowbanks are here—it'd come right over!"

Kevin called out, "Hey! It's comin' through!"

There were two places at the base of the snowbanks where the stream was coming through, as if tiny culverts had been run through the banks.

The boys left me at the bridge—that is, I did not invite them to the house (the kids were away, and I wanted to work).

To the left, between the pond and the road, was a sheet of water. The outlet to the pond was almost as high as the bridge, and looked like still water, since it reverses flow and takes in water from the stream. The beaver dam was entirely under water.

How desolate everything looked! Leafless trees and dead trees and the usual fat gray stumps of the bogs.

Enough snow had melted that the debris of many storms was now strewn together on the surface. A snowmobile trail going off into the woods (uphill, toward Esther Johnson's) at right angles to the road, was so strewn with evergreen debris that it was positively green.

I heard a roaring under the snow. A heavy, fast flow of water was rushing along both sides, completely hidden by the snowbanks, which functioned as tunnels and muffled the roaring yet made it more resonant, more hollow-sounding.

Late in the afternoon Hervey Andrews brought in Mabel and the kids in his pickup truck. He had seen them wading through the water—Mabel carrying Michael plus a knapsack of groceries. The water then was higher, almost eighteen inches.

MARCH 26

Gray; occasional rain, not much. The water has gone down a lot, but we probably can't get the Saab through the mud.

Peter Armstrong had offered to prune our apple trees—wanting to do something for Mabel, who has done so much for them.

He used a section of our aluminum ladder, bracing it against a tangle of tiny branches I would not have thought capable of holding it. Had a small pruning saw, small clippers. I carried some of the dead wood indoors for the fireplace.

Both small pear trees were dead of "fire blight," which makes them look burnt. I cut them both down.

Peter called from the apple tree: "You better haul them off a way, or burn them, the blight will spread to the apples."

Mabel dragged them both downhill.

I had made a small crude bow, arrows, quiver for Michael. He played with these and watched. Shem watched. The ponies came and watched. Poor Woody was chained to the porch, wretched after my harsh treatment of him of yesterday.

Peter said, "It's hard to keep the lower limbs in good shape. They're shaded too much, and the tree wants to grow tall. But then you can never reach the apples with a ladder."

I asked him about the scaling bark, if it should or could be scraped.

"Commercial orchards don't do anything about it, but I've seen people scrape it very carefully with a hoe. You have to be careful not to hurt the live bark underneath."

Nellie came home with Becky. Bob Kimber brought them to the bottom of our road and they walked the mile up, Becky with one very wet foot, as the water sloshed over her boot (my Wellingtons).

MARCH 30

Sunny morning. This is the time of maximum contrast between strips and patches of bare grass and areas of snow. High fields are bare already (and the wheel ruts of trucks and farm equipment can be seen)—the west sloping, and south sloping fields have much brown, matted dead grass in them. Northern slopes and slopes shaded by nearby hills still have a great deal of snow. There's still a foot of snow in most places in the woods.

Driving to Strong, mounds of firewood, that had been covered by snow, are now visible, and piles of junk, garden hose, toys, etc. that had been buried neatly under snow can now be seen strewn about. This is the time of maximum weather carnage—everything is bedraggled.

Along the Sandy River, where the river bed is wide and shallow and the banks are shallow, there's a strewn mess of ice slabs, up-ended, jumbled, over-lapped. A few damaged small trees—images, all this, of natural violence. How noisy it must have been when this ice started going!

One sees many dooryard sapping operations. A small sap house made like an arbor, with plastic over it—the usual fifty-gallon drum domestic evaporator, smoke stack. There seems to be more of this than ever, probably because the price of maple syrup has gone sky high. It's $2.60 a pint in the stores—the local stuff, in jars.

Mild spring breeze, moist with melting snow, cooled by melting snow (which happens to be my favorite temperature for beer).

Late afternoon the skies clouded over. I drove to Portland to meet Susie at the airport, and there was some rain on the way. By the time we got to the airport, it was raining hard, and we drove back through down-pours—until we reached Temple, where it wasn't raining and hadn't rained hard at all.

The poplar buds have opened.

April 3

It snowed a good bit of yesterday, a wet heavy spring snow—three or four inches. Today the eaves are dripping and the snow seems likely to melt soon. Gray skies. Fog.

Last year's beech leaves are a ghostly, translucent pale saffron, or even paler, almost an ivory but with a faint wash of salmon color. They looked like dried fish hanging from spits.

April 5

It began to snow late last night; now we have about four inches of wet heavy snow. It clings to the branches of the trees and piles up, even clings to the twigs of the trees—the stark *black and white* look, characteristic of this time.

Still snowing. Mabel couldn't make the hill in my Saab and parked down below, in the turn-around.

April 7

More snow yesterday, intermitted by sunshine. Today violent winds and a pale sun.

Snow melted from the roof and dripped, and the wind blew it violently against the windows, "shattered drops," a mottling of wet in all directions, little rivulets on the glass, to the accompaniment of whistling, roaring wind, blowing uphill.

Late afternoon there were flurries again, large flakes streaming great distances horizontally in the wind.

Dusk, wind still almost frighteningly strong.

Remarkable sight when gusts of wind divide the near mass of poplars at the edge of the road into two columns and set them swaying contrapuntally, so that when one column is bowing the other is straightening. Their feathery tops shift back and forth against each other.

APRIL 8

Flocks of starlings in a bare, brown field.

Sound of crows.

Sunny, windless, brisk.

Still lots of snow left in the woods and on slopes. Gray birch leaves are out. Red-wing blackbird sitting on a wire.

APRIL 9

Snowing again. White sky.

Snow all day.

APRIL 10

Mourning doves on the road to Strong. Bright ochre haze of the long, leafless stems of willows.

APRIL 12

Bright, windy, cold.

Sound of a chain saw.

Dogs and ponies sunning themselves, sprawled in brown grass, or porch. Woody likes to lie on a snowbank and catch the sun.

APRIL 13

At sunrise, after the sky is bright, but the sun hasn't cleared the horizon yet, hasn't yet cleared all the hills in the east, the valley and most of the hills in the west still have the cold blue/black shadows of night, but a land of evergreens is catching the sun in the valley and showing a bright dark green. Snow and bare ground, snow and black tree trunks.

Six Canadian geese fly by silently, due north. Why so few? I remember the stirring sound and sight of the migrating V's in the fall.

A crow flies across the Intervale, cawing.

The maple buds are thickening.

I went to the cabin for books and took the dogs with me. Some of the cabin road is clear, some under water, some under snow. Last year's leaves block the flow of water across the road, and open channels.

It's remarkable what a difference fifty feet in elevation makes. The upper stretch of the cabin road has a foot of snow in places, and so does the field by the cabin.

Blue sky today, a beautiful day so far (5:30–9:00). Some crow very noisy.

Yes, warm day of spring. Becky and Michael played outside without sweaters. Mabel lay in the sun—so did the dogs and ponies.

APRIL 14

Flock of starlings in the bare twigs of a medium sized tree—spectacular: 150 birds, or more.

Red tailed hawk.

Two ravens in a tree.

Two kestrels in a tree.

Early evening SNOW: By 1:00 am everything is white. I hear a partridge drumming.

APRIL 15—EASTER

Still snowing, big wet adhering flakes. Everything is white—the woods have the black and white look of a photograph—all the limbs, twigs, buds, and the just-opened leaves of the popples are white underscored with black. The evergreens are spectacular like this. A white sky. Prints of the dogs' and ponies' feet in the snow. Where the ground is muddy and wet, the snow melts, and here too is the stark black and white.

No wind. The flakes are heavy and fall straight down at a good speed; and they are numerous. The effect is a downward *streaming*.

The ponies paw away the snow and eat the brown grass.

While the snow falls, the eaves are dripping. Around noon the snow ceases and the dripping of the eaves increases until it sounds like a rainstorm.

Two hours after the snowfall ends, much of the ground is bare again.

A flock of thirty robins descends on our locust trees, and from there to the ground, where they dart about, listening, pecking. Sparrows with them. A crowd of grackles flies into the tree the robins just left.

The robins forage only briefly.

An hour later a fine rain is falling.

In the garden the chives are three inches high—tough and pungent, almost intoxicating to smell that fresh *green* after the long winter, and delicious in the vinaigrette Mabel made for the artichokes Aunt Frances sent us.

Two days ago we dug and ate the small crop of parsnips. These too were delicious. What one prizes is that taste of fresh-from-the-soil, though no doubt one is actually somewhat starved for certain minerals, enzymes, God knows what.

Rain, snow, rain, and by midnight it was snowing again.

APRIL 17

People taking down the plastic skirts from around their houses.

We can see how much dog and pony shit there is out front, out back, now that the snow is gone.

Gray and windy, but at least we can see across the valley.

Pot holes, frost heaves, crumbled asphalt, scars on roadside trees from the snow plow.

APRIL 29

A mild day, occasionally overcast.

There is increasing green along the road. The trillium is up, flowers ready to bloom. A lot of frog's-bellies and bracken and large helle-bore. The moss is refurbished, a bright green on rocks. Dandelion greens (no flowers yet). Still a few clumps of snow in the woods. Daffodils are up.

Night. The dogs are barking incessantly. Terrific pulsing volleys, screaming of the peepers, armies and armies of them screaming like huge crickets.

Moths have appeared in numbers, and there are mosquitoes in the house.

The long fronds of the willows have tiny leaves, pointed, the size of mouse ears, scattered along their lengths, bright yellowy-green.

The birches and poplars (females) drenched in long, bright green catkins.

APRIL 30

Flicker, trout lilies, barn swallow, daffodils.

A summer's day!

Helen and Nessa were here. Kick-ball, flying gliders from my bal-cony and Michael's toy parachute. Picnic lunch uphill on the big rock (the outcropping ledge). It was the day before Becky's birthday—Susie hid a little cake in the woods, and then after lunch, saying, "I have to go pee," she brought it, with candles, and surprised Becky.

Bumble bee (or Queen?) while we play.

MAY 4

A raven gliding across the valley.

Only the exhausted or shaded fields are still brown. There is green almost everywhere. A haze of green on the hills (scattered green), green on shoots and plants by the road, green in the fields. Farmers still manuring their fields.

MAY 6

Sunny, extremely windy.

Trout lilies and trillium both high and in full bloom along the cabin road. All the daffodils are blooming now, though the first were just up almost ten days ago.

People are picking fiddleheads.

Heard a loon in the morning, and saw two late afternoon flying over the bog toward Drury Pond.

MAY 8

Canoe, fiddleheads on Temple Stream. Ted says the streams are high, but this section is *much* lower than at this time last year. Our visiting German TV director came in the canoe with me, and the kids and I had to leap out often and pull it over sections we had sped across easily last year. It *is* possible that this entire stretch has silted up.

Saw a kingfisher here. The fiddleheads are well up, but will be more plentiful in a few days. There seem to be fewer than last year.

A few trout have been caught, not many.

Spring is well established now. There is bright yellow-green on the hills, small leaves on the younger maples, catkins on the yellow birch. Green grass, many roadside, pathside plants, mosquitoes. No black flies yet, but they'll be along in a few days. This is when the velocity and abundance of growth and change become unmanageable. One is swept along, changed with the changed.

MAY 9

Trout madness. The first time out is like a ritual. It is too early. Nothing works. But there is the flowing water of the large stream, so incredibly various in depth and bed—and there am I hopping from rock to rock. I fished the stretch near Elliot's old place. Caught one small one.

MAY 13

Caught a good trout and a small one in a brief outing on the stream by David Comparetto's house.

The avalanche has started moving: green, flowers, birds, bugs.

Black flies out now. Shadbush in blossom. Green everywhere. Baltimore orioles. Our barn is lively with swallows, and they swoop over the garden during the day—dolphins of the air.

Wasps searching—for nesting sites?

Plum trees in blossom.

Chores. Debris all over the yard: stones, tree limbs, pony and dog shit, balls, toys, old coffee pot, frisbee—stuff that was hidden in the long grass, then snowed under . . .

Light drizzle today.

I told Ted I had seen some white trillium—Janice Armstrong had been given some by her instructor at the college. Ted: "He probably lives in Chesterville then. That's the only place it grows around here."

MAY 17

Small leaves on the smaller locusts.

Air full of fluff from poplars.

Yellow dandelions everywhere.

Larger locusts still bare.

Cascades of blossoms on many apple trees. Also on plum.

Everything blooming, going too fast to see.

Two weeks ago I could see the cut wood (tops, etc.) by our road; now it's hidden in grass, ferns, shrubs.

Bob Kimber and I leave today for Holeb, Moose River, Attean— via Jackman. Back Sunday, God willing.

Lilacs.

[NEIGHBORS]

SLAUGHTERING THE SHEEP

Hanging head down, hooked through the tendons of the shins with clothesline.

Looking through the carcass, the November sun, the vaulted ribs and the rose lights of the flesh, like a cathedral.

The carcass hanging from the limb of the apple tree, the rippled ivory fat gleaming with the water they had swabbed over it with sopping rags. Rembrandt, Soutine.

"How quickly it becomes meat—and how good looking!"

The liver and kidneys, just pulled out, lay in the bucket on top of a pile of fat.

"You realize you're a carnivore when you look at things like that, fresh out of the animal, and they look good to you."

Laughs, "Yeah."

Chickens come, dogs come, the cat comes.

The liver is clean, dully glistening, of delicate, tender texture. The kidneys are clean, covered with a glistening membrane.

Splitting the head next day for my own dogs, cutting through the marvelous apparatus of brain and nerves with an axe. Pink ooze on the chopping block axe.

No food the night before, to reduce the quantity of shit that would have to be contended with. Cut around the anus, pull the tube of it up four inches, tie it with baling twine. Reach in and work a piece of twine behind and around the esophagus and tie it.

Bucket of hot water to wash the knives in so that they can be sharpened again. The wool takes down the edge in a few strokes. The scum of tallow on the blades; the greasy handles.

After the anus has been tied, and the penis and testicles removed, the stomach is slit open. One supports the great mass of the innards, the four stomachs, the intestines. The other reaches in and finds the bladder, surprisingly small, yet in its small way weighty with urine. The thinness and transparency of the membrane. This is dropped into the large tub. Now the vast membrane of the diaphragm, that divides the animal, sealing off the lungs and heart as in a separate room, is cut and removed. He reaches around the esophagus and ties it with twine. The windpipe has already been cut; the head is dangling loose. Now the soft, yet distended-firm, glistening, warm, slippery, clean, rounded, many-parted mass of stomach and guts is lowered into the tub, bringing with it the tubular openings at both ends, which have been tied. The tops of soft spheres crowded together (color: milky, fingernail-eye white), and long, soft, gleaming tubes coiled among them, all extremely warm and somehow inexplicable since they have been removed from their obviously elaborate functions. What has been left, dangling from the low limb of the apple tree, is the butcher's carcass of meat and bone.

He takes up the liver, severing it easily from the mass in the tub and removes the finger-like sac of bile, pinching it away from the healthy-looking cool magenta of the liver.

The warmth of the internal organs; lesser warmth of the meat but still noticeably warm to the touch—the day is chilly and brisk, yet is unseasonably warm for November.

Cutting the tendons in the forelegs—feel the twang of the shortening in my other hand, placed on the shoulder. The tendons, in their normal state, are stretched. When one end is cut, the tendon shortens. One can feel this recoil, this little snap, instantaneous and very strong, "muffled" in the flesh. So swift, like a nervous twitch, except that it's powerful, has impact.

Very little blood at any point.

The sheep were in the shed—three rams (one old), three ewes. When I arrived, Bob was straddling a dead sheep under the apple tree. He had just that moment brained it with the back of the axe and cut its throat. He held a front hoof between his knees and was cutting around the foreleg with his old hunting knife. I had brought three sharp knives and a stone. I held the other foreleg in similar fashion, cut all the way around the bony leg to begin the freeing of the pelt, then cut down the inside of the leg to meet Bob's cut just above the breast bone. He cut around the neck, meeting the deep gash on the throat at both ends. Back legs, belly, etc. "Punching" the pelt away from the fatty back. Laying the knife almost flat against the body so that the razor edge of it just lightly engages the receding bond of the wool-skin and the underskin, the former pulled back by the other hand. Creamy, milky colored fat—ivory skin suffused with rose lights (the blood beneath).

Bob straddled the live sheep, axe in hand, talking to it soothingly. When its struggling abated, he hit it toward the front of its skull with the back of axe. I held a rope around its neck, but loosely, in case it broke free, which happened with the second ram.

"This is the advantage of docking the tails. . . ." He cuts off the tail easily and throws it to the dog.

The stunned sheep lies motionless on the ground, but when Bob leans over and with pressing, sawing motions of the sharp knife cuts its throat, and the surprising gush of dark blood (a little of the paler venous blood mixed with it) appears, and the severed windpipe, severed cords, nerves, meat—when all this suddenly appears in that nest of thick "gray" wool, the unconscious sheep once again is terrified, and its legs gallop and thrust, five or six leaps that are like a dream.

Together (after it has bled—all over in a few seconds, not much blood) we drag it to the apple tree and skin it there. The chickens, cat, dog investigate the bloodsoaked grass where it died. A bluejay, too, comes to see what is happening, and there are six or seven sparrows.

The carcass is too heavy to lift without grasping it full around the body. Greasy. Bob, wearing old and ragged jacket, does this while I tighten the ropes that hold it to a limb of the tree. The ropes catch a bit on the rough bark and stubs of dead twigs, though the tree is alive, bore apples this year. A couple of frozen ones can still be seen on it.

I tell Bob of the gelding of Starbright, and how Chin-Chin had sniffed the testicles where they lay on the field, and then had trotted to the fence where the vet and I were leaning, had come to within eight feet of us and silently had bared her teeth at us, throwing back her head.

Sheet of fat, somewhat lacey, thin (quarter-inch), peeled back from the large stomach in the tub.

After the death of the ewe the remaining sheep were terrified when we entered the shed. "They smell the blood." We latched the door behind us and opened the door to the pasture, blocking the escape of the two rams that we wanted. The old ram and the two large ewes escaped. We caught one of the rams, feinting, anticipating its lunge— easy to grasp that thick wool though the ram was strong. Bob tugged it into a sitting position. "They're helpless in this position." I put the noose around its neck. Later, the other ram, more frightened than any, having been alone in the shed for two hours, stamped plaintively, not threateningly, in the corner. This one broke from Bob's grip outside, and struggled when Bob swung the axe, not a good blow; hit three or four times, but broke free and ran; I snubbed him with the rope; Bob seized and upended him again; I ran for the axe and we killed him there, brought him back to the blood-drenched place to cut his throat.

Bob in the shed talking soothingly to the last sheep standing there in the corner in terror . . . going slowly closer as he talked: ". . . Yes, just stay calm, poor thing, you know something's up, don't you . . . now just stay there . . . yes, just hold still, there's no place to go . . . that's a good sheep. . . ." Compassion in his voice, ominous death in that steady intent approach. Four days later, butchering the meat, we both praise it. "Oh boy, does that look good!"

Sawing the spine right straight down it. We washed the sections with warm water, carried them to the shed and hung them from nails on hunks of baling cord. Bob went to the house and locked in the cats.

"We've never done it so fast."

We took the six halves to Ellery, carried them *down cellar* and hung them in the refrigerator closet he built himself when he used to butcher and operate the little smokehouse.

EDDIE V

With the carolers, could see Eddie and Mrs. Swan through the window, staring at the TV, as if comatose, or as if watching the flickering of light and dark, not seeing actors and actresses. Someone knocked on the window. They didn't hear. Helen Blodgett knocked on the door, opened it, called to them. "Hi Eddie. We're going around singing carols. We'd like to sing you a couple." He stood there by the chair leaning on his cane, looking at her almost with alarm, sensing that something was wanted of him but not knowing what. Mrs. Swan was still staring at the set. We sang one carol and left, shouting *Merry Christmas,* and Eddie was still standing there, looking doubtfully at Mrs. Swan and doubtfully at the door. He couldn't hear the singing.

Mrs. Swan—round, or pyramidal, sitting in the easy chair, shoulders collapsed over her hips and belly—the soft, almost liquid flesh of extreme old age. Her cane lay across her lap.

Less than three weeks later she was dead. We didn't hear of it until after the funeral. I went down to pay my respects to Eddie and Nellie.

Nellie: "We thought everybody knew about it. She took sick with a cold and went to hospital. It turned into pneumonia. I guess she was just too old to fight it off. She was ninety-four, you know. Even so, it's been a terrible shock. People have been awfully nice about it. Everybody sent flowers. It was a well attended funeral."

Eddie: "Five hundred dollars worth o' flowers at the funeral. Even old Currier Holman sent flowers."

Nellie: "It was just a memorial service, you know. Yes . . . The burial will be in the spring of course."

Eddie (so I believe) had been fond of Mrs. Swan. She was sweet tempered and was grateful for services and attention. Eddie was able to do things for her, and be things for her, and this was important in his daily life, since he is a serviceable and actually a loving man. Now he's left with Nellie, who is bad-tempered, demanding, fault-finding, and impossible to please. Mrs. Swan had kept peace. Now anything could happen down there.

I talked with Eddie about his eyes. He had had the second operation, on the other eye, and still did not know how successful it had been.

"It hurts a lot. I keep wantin' t'scratch it. . . ."

Nellie: "You bettah *not!*"

Eddie: "Don't dare touch it. I can't lift anything. I can't even bend over, would put pressure on it. I can't go in the workshop. If the sawdust got in there, it'd be the end of it. I don't know how it is, I can't see much yet. You look pretty hazy to me. Lot o' black specks come out of it last night. Looked just like somebody'd sprinkled pepper on the pillow. I prob'ly hurt it at the funeral. It threw down a lot of water."

I asked him what he meant, "threw down water."

He said, "Tears."

His heavy, blocky, enduring style, yet he is sad, baffled. One feels he could sob like a child. All the *means* of independence, independent labor, have been taken away from him, and he's left with will and willingness floundering in a void.

Somehow we got to talking about the past. I said something about Slim Hodgkins.

Eddie (bitterly): "He was a slave driver. You couldn't turn your back on him. He could be nice enough if it wasn't business, but you had to watch him if it was. I worked for him three years. He was never satisfied. He'd work you from morning to night and then underpay you or owe it to you. He had the farm then. I milked the cows, cut wood, repaired things there in the store, then went and milked the cows again. You know that lot where his house sets? I cleared that lot. He paid me seven dollars a cord, and I fed my own hoss. I found out Mosher was payin' ten a cord and was supplyin' the hoss. We had words one night right there in the store. He said, 'I don't want no trouble with you!' I said: 'Then watch your mouth.' That was the last I worked for him a good long while."

"Moshers and the Hodgkins run this town. They got lots o' people to work for 'em just by loanin' money whenever it was asked for. Man'd be afraid to quit them then, be afraid t' cause trouble."

It seemed that Eddie hadn't spoken to anyone for a long time. It stirred his energy—surprisingly, and good to see.

"Don't hurry off. Come down again."

EDDIE VI

Eddie said the ice on Drury Pond was "lookin' black" and wouldn't last much longer. A windy day would break it up, and the wind would drive the pieces up on the banks.

I asked him if he'd ever cut ice on Drury. "No, but I cut some ice in New Sharon for Nellie's dad to put in his ice house. We cut from a gravel pit had filled up with water, it was easy to get to. We cut it in two-foot squares. We'd haul it up to the sledge by hand, two men and them big ice tongs. You'd make a long cut in the ice, and then a lot of short ones two feet apart at right angles to it, then the other long one, and take out the pieces. We'd mark the first cut with a rope and just sight in beside it by eye. The other cuts was just by eye. On a small job like that we'd use the old ice saw. Was about five foot long with them long curved teeth, more like steps than saw teeth, and the handle went crosswise so you could grip with both hands. But if you wanted to make time you'd use a chain saw. You'd file the riders off between the teeth and she'd cut ice slicker'n hell. You had t'wear a raincoat, though, she'd kick up a ton o' water right back on you! On a big job they had ice cutters. Them was circular saw blades, four-foot blades, driven by a gasoline motor and mounted on a frame, on runners. One man could push that frame by himself.

"After the sledge was piled up with ice, we'd haul it to the ice house. The ice house was sixteen by sixteen. We used a wooden sluice to slide the ice in. One man'd stay on the sledge, and the other'd be in the ice house with a rope with a pair o' tongs tied on the end, and he'd pull the blocks of ice right up that sluice and make one layer at a time. You had to get it started (he grabs an imaginary rope, smiling, setting his jaw for effort) but once you got it movin', she'd come right along pretty fast. You left about eighteen inches between the ice and the walls and you packed it all around with sawdust. Then you'd start your next layer, just ice to ice, no sawdust in between, and you'd go on like that till the pile was eight feet high, then you'd top it off with sawdust. That ice'd keep more'n a year like that.

"We was cuttin' one day over on Staples Pond and there was a man from out o' state standin' there watchin' us. He had a little dog beside him and the dog was wearin' one o' these little red dog blankets, or dog coats, or whatever it was. Well, a snowstorm come up, heavier'n hell, big flakes comin' down so thick you could just barely see. We'd took out a lot of ice so there was open water, but the snow was comin' down so fast the water was white. Well, that little dog had been movin' around, and damned if he didn't step right off onto that snow water. Disappeared. You couldn't see nothin'. We managed t' find 'im an' fish 'im out, and he come 'round all right, but that was one cold little dog."

They both laugh sympathetically, and Nellie says, "Poor little fella."

I ask Eddie if he's still making axe handles. He says, "I can't see to do it. I can see you all right sittin' there, but I can't see close up."

"Would special glasses help for that?"

"I don't know."

Nellie (sarcastically): "Nuthin' like askin'. . . ."

Eddie hates to deal with the doctors, hates to question them, or ask for anything. Is ashamed that he can't read.

He mentioned some other ailment. Nellie said, complainingly: "Failing, failing. . . . " and when he excused himself to go to the bathroom, she said, "Drip, drip . . . just drippin' away." I remembered his bitter hurt and hatred when he told me once it was "hellish" living with her. "Nothin' pleases her, nothin' is right. She can't stand herself and she can't stand nobody else."

We talk of the robberies, the marauding teenage boys. "They broke the windows out of Kike Knowle's trailer while he was away, and they unhitched his dog and the dog got run over." Flares with anger: "They break in up here . . . by God . . . I get my hands on a gun, I'll down 'em!"

Nellie: "Body can't sleep at night worryin'."

They ask, as always, after Mabel and the kids and listen attentively.

Flood warnings. Snow in Vermont and New Hampshire, but just rain in Maine. Nellie: "It's been a long slow winter. Not a bad one, but long and slow. I don't know . . . somehow it seems we been short o' sunshine."

THE CHRISTMAS PARTY

Miriam Kennison celebrated her ninetieth birthday a week ago. Helen Blodgett brought a cake for her. We sang Happy Birthday. After the party Dick Blodgett and I walked on either side of her, to help her out of the little red schoolhouse that now belongs to the Historical Society. The granite slabs that have been the steps forever aren't close to the threshold—much too long a gap for an old woman like that. We helped her across and she helped too with her cane.

She said, "You'd never know I went to school here. They're the same steps, too."

Dick said, "Yes, they are."

She said, "I didn't have such difficulty then."

Injuries, the unfailing topic. *This* conversation never occurred in New York. We would hear of its opposite—suicide.

Bob Stevens, telling how his son lost a finger all the way back to the thumb, on the wood splitter. He was working alone and was pinned in it for fifteen minutes until someone came, and then he had to hold a wedge while the other man used a sledgehammer. He had been split-ting "both ways," i.e., on the return cycle, too. He milks forty cows and wasn't able to work for five or six weeks after the amputation. Bob Stevens did the milking for him.

Talk of "phantom limbs." So-and-so, who'd lost his leg, scratching at his pants, where there wasn't any thigh. I said, "What are you doin', Ralph?" He said, "My leg is itchin'—it's about to drive me nuts."

"Oh yes—dad has the first joint of his finger off. He says it drives him up the wall when it itches—there's nothin' he can do."

Dick showed the finger he'd caught on the table saw. "I took the end right off on the diagonal. I told the doc, 'Take it off,' but he said no, it might heal. Well, it did . . . I mean it looks all right, but it's numb, there's no feeling in it. When I'm hammering nails, I'll swing, you know, and gosh, there won't be any nail there. I can't tell whether I'm holdin' one or not."

Bob Stevens told about the pro wrestlers he hired when he was raising money for a recreation center. "They were all good friends, you know. They'd come down in two cars, then they'd stop outside of town and rearrange things so nobody would see them coming in with the guys they were going to fight. It was all fake, of course—but they took real falls, you know. They're in good shape, those guys. They'd spend a whole hour in the locker room getting warmed up. I asked one of them—this was before the days of long hair, but he had hair down to here, he called himself Chief Hungry Wolf, but he was an Italian kid from the Bronx. I said, 'How can you do this fake stuff? How can you go through it?' He said, 'Number one, it's not fake—we know who's going to win, but when I get thrown across the ring, I get thrown across the ring. I have to land just right. He has to throw me just right. I can drop you from over my head if you want to see what it's like. Number two . . . can we see your car from the door here? Which car is yours? That old Ford there? That one? Yeah? You see that new Cadillac at the corner? That's my car. Get it?'"

Not much gaiety this year, everyone a little blue, preoccupied, tired. Jean and Ron Mitchell remembered their son who was killed on the highway a few months ago, and who was home to see them last year at this time. And Ron's father, who they had been fond of, died recently. And there have been other deaths, and there are some old folk who are close to the end. Cards are sent to absent members, and to an elderly woman who is in the hospital. "I guess she's not doing so well"—it means she's expected to die.

And everyone had to get up early and go to work. Sentimental songs—*Rudolph* ugh!—no one even knows the Christmas carols! Lives of hard work, endurance, outdoor things.

It all peters out, people drifting away to their homes. But *still,* there were good moments and good feeling, an underlying friendliness.

DICK BLODGETT IV

We drove in his truck up the old Avon Road—or one of the several "old Avon roads"—that goes along Temple Stream, and that I used to walk when I visited Ted when he lived on the mountain "back in the old days." When Dick talked about the "old days," however, he meant fifty-five years ago, forty years ago . . . not the fifteen that I meant.

The road was in good shape.

"Who's cutting in here?"

"Well, Mosher is. . . ."

"Oh? Where's he cutting?"

"Well, right along here . . . straight up there. Vilio and the boys are workin' with him. Gosh, I shouldn't say *boys* anymore, Joanne's cuttin' right along with 'em, good, too.

"This used to all be fields in here. The Jenkins place was right here. Good-sized place, too. Oh if you look around, there's cellar holes all through here. Back there in that flat place there was a pretty good settlement. A lot of Welches back in there. They moved down to West Farmington, to the place they call Clay Hill. Doctor Little's place was all open when he bought it. I put the metal roof on the barn for him . . . that was just twenty-five years ago. You could see right through here and see the Kennison place up on the hill. That was a nice farm. My grandad worked on that place. I used to go up there with him while he was shinglin' it. We'd hitch up a horse and go in the morning. Lots of times I'd end up stayin' with him. I spent a lot of time with him. He was a wonderful man. He was a tremendous man. He could do just about anything. He played the fiddle and made furniture and built houses and sheds and barns and fences and gates. He could do apple trees—graftin', y'know—and he knew all about bees. People talked about him a long time after he died. I was eight years old when he died. I'm sixty-one now, so that puts it back a ways, but I can see him so clear, just as if he was standin' there. He died of a stroke. You know the old Parker place way up above Mitch's? Nice high fields and an orchard. He was working there when it happened. He was hurt too bad to move. The doctor come out. There wa'nt no hospital back in them days. I suppose if it happened today and it wasn't too bad, they could help you a lot, but back then if that happened to you, you was a goner. He hung on for three days. They took me up to see him before he died."

Hartley Farmer has twelve cows. He made an arrangment with Dick to hay the big field at Rosie's place. The flood ditches put in by the state made it impossible to drive onto the field from the main road, but Dick told him to take a chain saw and cut an overhanging apple limb and go in from the driveway to the house, past the trees.

We saw someone mowing in there as we set out to go fishing. It had rained already and was raining again. The man climbed off the tractor and ran to his truck. Dick and I drank beers in *his* truck and looked at the field. "Hartley'll be hurtin' for hay," he said. "It doesn't look long enough to cut, and there's not much to it. He spent six hundred dollars on fertilizer. I don't believe he'll get his money back." Later he said, "It should've been plowed up and seeded. There's no use fertilizin' weeds." Still later he talked about the hay at Isalo's place, where he and Helen live now. He said people often baled their hay so wet now that it burned up to nothing. Isalo "farmed the hard way. The Finn way. It was all by hand, you know. He cut it before it headed, and before any weeds might have gone to seed. But you couldn't find a weed in it. He didn't bale it, you know, he packed it in the barn by hand. It lasted almost forever."

I said that I remembered how much green was in the hay he had given me several years ago, and it had been fifteen years old. He said yes, he had given a lot of that hay to Elmer Swale and the cows had eaten it right up. Dick had cleaned out the barn after Isalo died. Isalo hadn't kept cattle in his extreme old age, and so the hay had gotten old.

"He used to do an acre a year, plow it and seed it. Every five or six years it would come around again. Wa'nt that good hay! He had the best lookin' hay around! Ayuh."

Dick Blodgett V

After poker, talking with Dick:

He had spoken, during the game, of Dr. Mitchell, who had grown up here in Temple, had prospered simply as a country doctor, and had left a couple of hundred thousand dollars to the town—in 1930's dollars. He had endowed a room at the hospital to be used by Temple residents, and had made some other arrangements, which hadn't been met very well by the banks and lawyers involved. Dick said, "He and my grandad had been real close, and he was always real fond of my father. He used to write him the nicest letters, always addressed to Harvey Blodgett, Esquire. I got a kick out o' that. I asked mother if she'd saved them letters, but she hadn't. They was written so nice, you know, such nice penmanship." Dick had a copy of the will, and had just made a copy for the selectmen. He had shown his copy to Peter Mills, the lawyer, and Peter was going to study the question of its execution. Dick remarked on how surprised people were by the quantity of money involved—that he had made so much. I asked Dick if Dr. Mitchell were related to Ronnie, etc., but Dick said no, the relationship was closer to the Blodgetts.

George and Charlie and Larry—bad feeling because of the union. Dick was saying that George is popular but in a position to be fired because foremen get fired. He is Larry's foreman, and Larry has been there twenty-five years. "I've been worried about that"—this was his way of apologizing for George's being "on the wrong side of that," i.e., being against the union because he's salaried. "The company expects George and Charlie to put pressure on the men that want a union. But I know George didn't.

"Knowing that company, I worry about it. Jules worked there all his life. He put in long hours and was highly skilled and that helped his social security a lot. But then when they asked him to come in and help out, they dropped his pay way down, same as they'd pay an unskilled part-time worker. He didn't want that."

"Hanrahan, the warden, goes out with a trained Doberman. Bud Olson was poaching smelts, and Hanrahan got after him, but the brush was there and Hanrahan fell and broke his glasses and lost his pipe, so he said the hell with it and put the dog on his trail. About five minutes later he could hear Olson's voice: 'Git this goddam dog off me.' That dog had run him right up a tree. The dog is trained to do that. If Hanrahan had said, *sic him,* instead of *tree 'im,* the dog would have chewed him to death. Some day somebody will shoot that dog. I know if I was up a tree with my thirty-aught, I'd sure as hell blow his head off.

"There's supposed to be six or eight dogs like that in the state now. Some o' them are trained to smell deer meat."

Dick, after the game, talked about his mother, and his own ailments, which he rarely does. He has been taking pills for his heart and to keep his weight down. "My blood pressure was so high I was prob'ly right close to a stroke. But the medicine has brought it down good, and I'm still losing weight, though it doesn't look to me that there's a lot left to lose."

Florence totally blind now. Dick said of the young doctor: "I didn't think much of him. He's not too impressive." Told of having to ask the three doctors to please coordinate their examinations rather than force his mother to travel so far so many times, since travel is extremely difficult and painful. He didn't like the way the young doctor spoke of her in her presence, or the fact that the outside stairs to the doctor's office had an extremely long last step, impossible for someone moving on crutches.

"You'd think he'd have a ramp, but I don't believe he was even aware of it." This was the doctor who had tried the laser treatment, which had cost $600 and had failed totally.

"She has to be tended around the clock now. Cindy Tyler's been staying with her. She's doin' a real good job. Mother's very demanding now. She's frightened, you know, and she's depressed. I'm trying to get her to try one more operation. They say there's a chance for her, but she doesn't seem to believe there is, and that's not good."

Since the laser, she sees a white light that hurts her—sees it when her eyes are closed.

Dick (continuing the talk about his heart): "I have these black-outs, you know, and the doctor doesn't know what to make of 'em. I have 'em fairly frequently, several times a week, but I can feel 'em comin' and stop what I'm doin', pull over if I'm drivin', or just sit down and rest. I was layin' a pine floor a couple of days ago down Chesterville, nice wide boards, fine boards. They'd been planed on both sides, but with something that wide there's going to be a certain warping, so I had to plane the edges pretty often, and I had to buck 'em in good to get 'em to fit. There was a young fella helpin' me, but them was heavy boards, and I could feel the black-out comin'. I said, 'I'm going to have to get outside and sit down.' He said, 'Are you all right?' I said, 'Oh yeah. I'm okay. There's nothing to worry about, but I've got to get some air and sit down a while.' I call 'em the Barker fit, because it's run in the Barker family. And I don't know, sometimes I think it's partly mental. Sometimes I get awfully depressed. I feel like things are closing in on me, then I want to be alone and just go for a walk. I'll get up in the middle o' the night sometimes and just walk up and down the road here. It always passes. Don't last too long."

I went down to visit with Florence in her nicely kept and nicely roofed mobile home. Helen Blodgett was there, and Cindy Tyler. Florence lay on the sofa making sounds of pain and touching her ear. A crutch leaned against a nearby chair. She reminded me of my mother—the same dignity, strength, and modest simplicity. Helen told me Florence's ear had been hurting her terribly. I spoke to Florence. She responded with great friendliness and graciousness—the latter not formal, she's unaware of it, as she's unaware of her dignity. She knows that she's being courteous and a little reserved in a general way, but the other qualities are unconscious. Helen came back from the phone and said, "He says he can look at you now if you come in right away." Florence said, "It will be rugged for me, but I suppose I can do it."

Old people so often seem like what is basic in humanity. So much of the vanity and dishonesty of careers has fallen away, they are no longer fiercely attached to their own opinions—one sees virtues and sweetness and compassion and the desire to do something useful and something interesting. They and children.

I helped Florence get out of the house and into the car. All three of us had to assist her. Her legs are crippled badly by arthritis, the knees twisted toward each other and neither leg very well aligned below the hips. She moves with pain, must use a crutch and must be assisted. The total blindness is recent. She must be guided every inch of the way, since she needs one hand for the crutch and the other to hold on to someone for balance. "Now there's a little tiny step right under the toe of your shoe. Move Amos first, just about six inches, and duck your head just a little." So sounds Helen. Amos is the crutch.

Florence muttered once a response to the pain and nuisance of it all. We had already commented on how much better it would be if the healthy young doctor could come to *her*. When I heard her moan, I said, "Well Florence, those guys have to earn a hundred thousand a year, and it's up to us to help them all we can." She said, "Lord yes."

DICK BLODGETT VI

After the poker game he and I drank some more and talked.

I: "The town has changed a lot in the last ten years. . . ."

Dick: "Oh it has! I see faces at the town meetin' I don't know *who* they are! And there's this little development right down the hill here, I don't believe I know a single person in it."

I: "When I first came up here thirteen or fourteen years ago, I used to hike all over the hills back here, but I feel different about it now. . . ."

Dick: "Ayeh . . . you feel you're walkin' on somebody's property. I used to walk around a lot myself, but it seems all built up now, even though there's not near's many people as there was. . . ."

I: "Temple has a complicated history. All the Finns—they came and went, there aren't many left."

Dick: "Yes, I knew old Vic. He was a fine fellow. But there were people right here in town didn't know who he was."

DICK BLODGETT VII

Dick and I drank beer and vodka and talked in his kitchen. George, Charlie, Ronnie, Vilio were at the Fair. Usual jokes: well we're not makin' much money, but we're not losin', either.

We spoke of aging—injuries, loss of strength, weight, health. I had ruptured a calf muscle playing tennis, was told it would need six weeks to heal. I always hesitate to mention my sport injuries among people whose injuries are inflicted on their onerous jobs and are often truly severe. Talking alone with Dick I mentioned it.

Dick: "I used to weigh a hundred and eighty-five. There were times when I went over two hundred, but I was never fat. I had real good legs, real strong legs. I carried a lot of weight on my legs. But my muscles are all gone. I weigh a hundred and sixty now. The doctor says that's good—but my muscles are all gone. It happens fast, just in the last few years."

Grandson: "You're fat now. Your stomach hangs over your belt."

Dick: "Well, I guess it does, you little devil."

I: "These kids are ruthless. I get that from Michael and Becky. Susie is old enough now to understand that I have to be treated kindly." Dick actually is quite trim. The overhang is small.

My ruptured calf, the ruptured muscles in my forearms the time I had to paddle against the wind on the West Branch using the big kayak paddle—five hours upstream against a heavy snow-filled October wind, either that or be blown all the way down to Chesuncook Lake and worse trouble still—though I could have made shore and waited it out. The tendonitis in both arms from heaving cord wood—fifty or sixty pound pieces—onto a truck all day, not being used to that kind of thing. My diastasis rictus—kayak paddle; my beginning hernia; my stiffness that might be arthritis, etc.

Dick has emphysema, and heart trouble, for which he takes medication. He drinks too much, never has been able to sleep well. Helen was there for a while. She complained—in her way that is both serious and joking, or "as if," a way that says, "This is true and I feel it, but you don't have to take me seriously"—that she could hear the electric fence bleeping on Dick's radio at night! Dick laughed and said, "I sleep with the radio goin'. Always have. I use little earplugs I stick right in my ears so as not to keep Helen awake."

"But sometimes I hear it anyway. Golly!"

"I'll wake up and listen to the news. I'll be awake half the night."

I mentioned that Becky and Michael were working as volunteers at the Common Ground fair, in Windsor this year, and that both were walking around on stilts now. Dick: "Oh, I used to do a lot of stilt-walking. We made the kind that came up under your arms and you held onto. But they were quite high. I'd say my foot was about as high as this ceiling. I could step across Lynch's brook with one step. We made them out of spruce poles. They were light and strong. We'd put a strap over the foot. That was a big help, and you weren't caught in it in case you fell; you could get your feet out all right. Sometimes we'd toss down one stilt and see how long we could hop around just on one. I was good at it. I had to get into a tree to get on the darn things. I used the apple tree just this side o' dad's place, that pie tree in the yard."

Horse racing. Charlie had come in from 4-H chores at the Fair, where his daughter—seventeen—had exhibited a beef animal. Charlie said that even after deducting the cost of the grain and other expenses, she made $700 on it this year; $500 last. All the trots are fixed, they both maintained. There had been a brawl after the horsepulling, about fifteen guys whaling the hell out of each other, bottles flying. "They finally got it under control. Junior Judson said, 'I held down three o' them, and Harry pulled off a few.' Did you ever see Junior Judson? He stands about six four and weighs well over three hundred. His arms are the size of legs. He's fat, but there's lots of muscle in there too."

Rickie (ten or eleven years old) was there. We talked about the pig scramble. They hadn't won a chance this year. Last year Kirk's name had been chosen and he had grabbed a pig (he is only five or so, but rugged and high tempered)—the pig had dragged him all around but he hadn't let go, and they had raised the pig. Rickie talked about carrying grain. "I can carry a fifty-pound sack, but a hundred's a bit too much."

Dick told of doing chores once for a farmer while he was in the hospital. He had to carry hundred-pound sacks of grain quite a distance from the main road to the barn. There were several cows. Cut wood, etc. It was heavy work and there was a lot of it. "I worked in the woods a lot with dad too. I liked workin' in the woods. We could do four cord a day. That was four dollars, a dollar a cord. Course you cut it with bucksaw or the crosscut in those days, there wan't no chainsaws. Usually you brought it down with the crosscut, and if the tree was big you might work it up with the crosscut, otherwise you'd work it up with the bucksaw. We'd fell a lot o' them so they held each other off the ground, then we'd go through them with the bucksaws usually, or the crosscut if they was big. It's surprisin' how fast that crosscut could go. There was quite a rhythm to it. You got so you couldn't even feel the man on the other end. If you could feel him at all, you wasn't doin' it right. Dad and I could do four cord like that. There were men who could do five. Most could just do one. Even with a chainsaw most men today can just do five. They'll tell you they can do ten, and there are a few that really can, but most can just do five.

"The wood wasn't skidded out in those days. We stacked it right there in the woods and then loaded it on drags. Most of the work was done in the winter. We had a sledge drag could take a cord crosswise. We cut a pine once that just two sticks fitted in lengthwise. There was some girth on that pine. It wasn't as heavy as what you might think. Pine's a light wood. But often, when we had big birch or rock maple, the two of us together would be loadin' sticks that weighed seven eight nine hundred pounds apiece. You never hefted that weight. You couldn't. There was ways o' doin' it, you slid it and rolled it, and wiggled it—you had to have just the right timin', and you didn't want to let go of it, you didn't want to let it fall . . . gosh no."

Dick had some pine milled for him at Smiley's mill in New Sharon, a small mill. "He's very particular about havin' the wood clean. Those saw blades he uses are very expensive."

"I've been told that the chief purpose of the old mill ponds was to clean off the wood. . . ."

"Well no, I wouldn't say that. The wood wasn't skidded out in those days. It was piled on drags right there at the stump. And the wood wasn't *stored* in the pond, it was stacked up beside the mill. Sometimes they had a channel to lead the logs into the saws. An o' course the water kept the wood from checkin'. But no, the main purpose was to keep up a head of water for the wheel. The wheel wasn't all that big, only like this, maybe (five or six feet). It was amazin' how much power came from it, enough to turn all that machinery in the mill. There was two shifts workin' around the clock. Twelve hours on, twelve off. They had to do all they could while the water lasted. Once the streams went back to normal, you couldn't saw."

Dick was working in his little shop when I arrived. He showed me the sconces he was making for the old schoolhouse—contributing his labor. They were wonderfully well done, like everything of his. Good proportions, good work, modest and handsome, never glossed-up or pretentious.

He had made a simple little table for the router. "You can buy these," he said, "but I don't buy that kind o' thing, I always make it. Don't look like much, but it does the job and that's what it's for . . ."

DICK BLODGETT VIII

Dick Blodgett and Toby talking about trees. Toby had just hauled out a fine large pine through Rosie's back fields, and measured the diameter with a yardstick. It was thirty inches across, straight and free of knots. I asked Dick if he was buying pine (he was there by our bridge simply to check the route for Toby), and he said, in the bantering style one hears here, "Oh not this stuff, it's nothing but knots and red heart. There's no wood on this."

Toby: "You might get a two by four out'n it."

"Oh yeah, prob'ly git three or four."

A moment later both were praising the tree, and Dick was telling of the fine pine he and his dad had hauled out of that back woodlot years ago with horses. He told how many cord and units and then the number of trees, this by way of indicating their size. Same with birch. "The first birch we hauled out of there was twenty-eight across. We hauled." Toby told of some birch he and his dad had cut on the mountain, how tall it was before the first limb.

Dick (later, pointing to the outlet beyond the bridge): "I used to get pickerel in there when I was a kid. Used to hit 'em with a club. I got quite a few that way. They wouldn't bite at all. You couldn't get 'em to bite. They'd lie right up close to the surface, oh just two or three inches down (shows with fingers). You'd take a club like that stick there and just give 'em a whack."

DICK BLODGETT IX

We fished on Temple Stream from Doctor Little's place down. Dick went up to the bridge at Ted's old place. For two miles there's nothing but a few camps and woods. At one place, half a mile before Doctor Little's, Dick said, "There used to be a schoolhouse right in there somewhere. That was before my time, but this used to be a well populated place."

We fished some pools close to the road. "People used to call this 'the ledges'—we used to have picnics here. Look at all the initials— see? Look. It's a pretty place. I guess it's pretty well fished out, but usually somebody pulls a couple of good fish out of it every year, maybe a little earlier than this.

"There didn't used to be many fishermen, you know. Just two or three in the whole town. Nobody had the time or money to do it. If you were workin' for a dollar a day and tryin' to raise a family, you couldn't be runnin' off to fish. Dad used to work in the woods. He got paid sixty cents a cord, and a day's work was two cords . . . ayeh . . . that's a lot of wood cut with a bucksaw. Same with hunting. Nobody had time. You couldn't just go off and do it. When dad and I did get a chance, though, it wasn't hard to catch fish. The limit then was twenty-five a day, and if we worked a section of stream like you and I just done, we'd have twenty-five with no trouble.

"Late in the day like this the trout will be down at the end of the pools feeding. They won't be up in the fast water."

Dick showed me the stream very much in the spirit of a host. He likes to talk about the past. Some sense of death in this.

THE CEMETERY

Work party at Hamlin cemetery, cutting brush that had grown up around the graves. The growth is enormous in one year. Last year we cleared out trees and brush both. Hartley said it might be better to spray it and then seed it.

Hartley: "There must have been a real nice view from here before those trees grew up. (To Dick.) You must've been up here when it was still open, eighty, ninety years ago. What was it like, Dick?"

"Well I was lookin' down from heaven. Yeah, it was nice."

Dick: "Yeah, I was the last one to cut the grass up here, in '39. . . ."

Hartley: "Why didn't you keep up with it?"

Dick: "Course a sprat like you wouldn't be aware of it, but we had a war goin' on back then. Heatin' up, anyway . . . No, I cut all the fields up here for Luther Hamlin. It was all pasture up here, but the farm was down below. Do you know Mr. Fife, the blacksmith? Yeah . . . well he said to me one day, Wasn't that a shame what Luther Hamlin done to himself, hanged himself and all. And I said, No, it wan't. If I'd known he was goin' to do it I'd've helped him. And old Fife draws back and says 'Why?!' And I said, The man was a crook. He cheated me and he cheated everybody. I worked for him right after I got out of high school, cuttin' hay and milkin', anything at all that came up, and I could cut with the best o' them. Got a dollar and a half a day, seven dollars a week. At the end o' the first week he gave me three dollars. I said, 'What's this?' He said, 'I'll pay you the rest next week,' but then next week he handed me five dollars. By the time I quit workin' for 'im, he owed me a hundred dollars. That was a lot o' work. And he died owin' it. And that was on top of money he owed me from before, while I was still in school. As soon as school let out for the day, I'd go to the Farmer's Union and get two bags o' feed. I had to carry it in by hand. I could take two sacks at once in those days, I was rugged. Then I milked eighteen head by hand, and I brought up ice for the tank. I did that for several months, 'til school let out for the year and I could work full time somewhere, so I went to him to settle up. He said, 'How much you want?' I said, 'Seventy-five cents a day.' He said, 'Well . . . I wasn't figurin' on payin' more'n fifty . . . ' I said, 'Oh?' and he said, 'Yeh.' So I said, 'Well then, you don't owe me nothin'. I don't want your money.' I was a fool to go to work for him ever again. But when you're young like that, it's hard to believe that a man can be so crooked. And it's hard to hold a grudge."

"Was he related to Dana?"

"Oh yeah, they was brothers. Dana didn't like to pay money, either, but he wasn't like Luther. He died owin' me money, too."

"I haven't smoked for two weeks. It's drivin' me up the wall. I have a carton at home, and I keep the lighter in my pocket . . . maybe that's not so smart, though. I took one o' those stress tests and they found some kind o' problem with my heart. They had me runnin' on a treadmill and they kept increasin' the slope. Well, I don't jog or anything like that, so after about eight minutes I was tired, so I said, 'Doc, I'm gettin' off this thing, I've about had it.' He said, 'No, keep goin'.' I said, 'Oh, I don't think so. I've had enough.' I was staggerin' around when I got off it. They said my performance wasn't bad, in fact it was at the upper end of pretty good. And they said the emphysema wasn't hurtin' much. But they found something wrong with my heart, and the doctor said, 'You better quit smokin'.' So I said, 'You're tellin' me the same thing my wife tells me, and my son, and my grandchildren.' He said, 'You better quit.' So I said, 'Well it's time I listened to 'em, so I guess I will.' And I *have* . . . but my *God,* I've been goin' through hell."

He saw me sharpening the brush scythe. I thought I was doing it pretty well. He laughed and came over. "Gosh, we'll never make a farmer out o' you. You better stick to writin', George."

"Am I doin' it wrong?"

"Well, yes. . . ."

He took the scythe, turned it 180°, put his arm over the blade, lengthwise, and sharpened it with short strokes on both sides, two kinds of strokes, a grinding stroke, and a long one.

I: "Did you ever put on an edge by hammering it?"

Dick: "No, we usually took it down with the grindstone, on the wheel, you know, and then just touch it up. . . ."

Hartley: "The best method is to take it to Jules and let him do it."

Hartley and Bob Stevens had power cutters. There were three or four brush scythes. The women raked, or used the long-handled nippers. Hartley's boys, a boy related to Ron Mitchell, and Michael were there. They used the nippers. They built a fire at lunch time and roasted hot dogs. Hartley's boys were very friendly toward Michael, and very courteous and considerate.

I said, "One disadvantage of our little school is that Michael probably misses out on making new friends."

Dick: "Oh, I don't know. Ricky and Dana don't have friends. I keep askin' 'em if they've made any new friends. But they really don't. They talk on the bus, but once school's out for the day, that's pretty much it. People live too far from each other. That's probably the whole story right there."

Melanie examined the graves to see if she had missed any soldiers of the revolution in her previous search. These graves have some kind of marker, a bronze flag or something. She did find one she had missed. There are three.

Dick: "What I can't figure is why are we *doin'* this? They don't care. They been dead a long time. You goin' to clean things up for me, Hartley, after I'm gone?"

Hartley: "Well, if I hear you expressin' discontent, Dick, I sure will. You revolutionary soldiers ought to be cared for."

Dick: "To say nothin' o' the Civil War, and the War of 1812, and all them others. Us old men have been through hell, I can tell you. But you wouldn't understand, Hartley. People your age think war is just a television program."

Hartley: "Do you like smoked fish, George? I built a smoke house last year and did some ham and bacon. I might try some fish this year. We got a batch of good size suckers last spring. We cut nice fillets off them and deep fried them, but they was awfully bland. I think if I smoked them it might bring out the taste. I'd prob'ly use alder for that. I used cherry for the pork, kept it in five days. I asked my uncle Ellery how long to smoke it and he said, 'Oh, 'til it gets to a good color.' I said, 'Well Ellery, what in the hell's a good color?' He said, 'Oh, not too light, not too dark, just a nice color.' He said the same thing when

I dug my bean hole. I said, 'How deep should I make it?' He said, 'Deep as you want it.' And I said, 'Then what?' 'Oh, put a few stones in if you like.' 'And how long do I leave the bean pot there?' 'Why, 'til it's done!'"

[J O U R N A L]

APRIL 5
Slow-moving wasps in the sun.

Cold-drugged wasps in the old attic dormitory. Dick and Hartley sealed in an old nest when they insulated the front room in the attic.

APRIL 15
Geese in a lopsided V, going north. Seen twice this week.

APRIL 19
A chickadee hits the window and dies. Heard the concussion. Susie found the little body. All the children looked at it. It lay on its back, clean and pretty, its two small legs sticking straight up, the claws curled back, each perfectly duplicating the other.

"Couldn't it see the window?"

"The clouds and sky are reflected there today."

I tell about the partridge that broke a window at Doctor Little's. It was dazed and its head was bloody (inside, on the floor—I saw it hit and go through). I was able to open the window and climb in. I carried it out and put in under some bushes. It recovered, and ten minutes later was able to fly away.

APRIL 21
A partridge drumming most of the night near my cabin—compressed air drumbeats, at first large, round, and slow, becoming smaller, rapid,

and sharper. When I first came to these parts and heard it, I thought I was hearing an ancient motor in the distance, starting hesitantly, "grabbing," then gathering speed. I walked around the cabin at daybreak. A huge male partridge flew away powerfully from a sunny mount of rock, not forty feet from the cabin. I think he had been drumming there in the night—the sound is that deceptive.

A small bird, but bigger than a chickadee, hit the glass in my cabin door—a good *thump,* but it survived and flew away.

APRIL 22

A sunny day, our first real day of spring.

Michael six days out of the cast, getting around with great spirit but limping quite badly. He tires easily (but recovers quickly) and can't go rapidly over rough terrain. I come down from the cabin and hear voices in the south field, then see Becky with Michael in her arms, straight up, like a big sack, hugging him, carrying him down toward the sauna.

APRIL 28

Michael and I went back to the beaver dam. We looked at the stump and skid trails.

On a one-inch yellow birch there were about forty chisel marks (but each bite makes two marks) the beaver had gone through it that fast. On a three-inch (alder? popple?) there were about 120 separate bites.

The chips lie all on one side (is it the downhill side, as I think?), as if the animal had reached around and cut back towards itself, pulling off a long chip, that represented eight chomps or so, which it dropped near its feet. This is speculation to fit the appearances.

I examined one of the long chips. The beaver seemed to have cut right through top and bottom, and to have pulled it away all through the middle.

The twelve-inch popple had chips all around it, though much more on the downhill side. Perhaps with a tree that big the beaver is obliged to move around it, which seems more likely than that several work on it at once. This was a fodder tree. They topped it and limbed it and maybe carried that stuff off to the lodge and dam. But the long piece of the big trunk lay where it fell, and they had already eaten half the bark. Probably with a tree that big—on which the bark grows coarse near the base, they just eat from the upper parts.

Their new dam went from shore to clumps of earth, over gaps again to earth again, and so on across the water and marsh of the inlet end of Drury Pond. Their new pond is already two feet higher than Drury; *its* height, too, is controlled by another dam on the outlet.

Their lodge—about seven feet above water level, with many sticks bristling out of the packed mud (some sticks as thick as an arm)—stood just five or six yards from the dam, and eight or nine yards from the shore.

Michael and I walked parallel to shore, on a deer trail. I was wearing hip boots. I helped him walk out on a log—he jumped in and had a *very brief* swim in the icy water. The pond has been free of ice for only a week. But this was our first *hot* day.

APRIL—TWO YEARS LATER

Rain and melting late snows—high water warnings. And then a week later a heavy all-night rain—and our lower road is badly flooded.

The woods have been free of snow but there's still ice in the ponds, except close to shore.

Much new beaver work near the inlet to Drury Pond, between the old mill race and the pond—a new lodge, a new dam underway. Stumps of all kinds and all sizes on slopes near the dam—bare earth skid trails where they've dragged the tree trunks down to the water. The stumps are pointed all around, and show the broad chisel marks of their teeth. At the base of each stump but entirely on one side lie the loose piles of chips, orange in their fresh state—each chip half an inch wide, or three-quarters or one-inch, and a good three inches long.

They had cut poplar, alder, ash, even striped maple. One of the poplars was a foot or more in diameter. This long trunk *was used as food*. It lay there on ground, the bark half gone.

I saw a cut tree—an ash five inches in diameter, tall—cut but hung up—and the beaver had started another cut above the first one, to free it, just as a lumberjack would. This work was unfinished. All over these slopes there was unfinished work. Either my presence had sent them all into hiding, or this was where they left off when they all went home to sleep from the night shift.

June 30

Tasha and Teebo are large pups now, and are like a free-moving musical comedy, rushing headlong into everything, and always in unison, even to the turning of their heads, the pricking of their ears, and the wagging of their tails.

My fishing trip:

I wanted to go down to the pickerel pond (Meadow Pond) with my fly rod and get some experience using it on pickerel. I had bought a new line—mounted it on the spool, took hip boots in my hand, smeared bug repellant all over me, and went off into the woods—slow going because of the summer growth, but so I came to the shallow, reedy pond, and put on the hip boots. I heard a crashing in the undergrowth, saw a brownish dog that looked familiar, then another—the pups had picked up my trail. They came hurtling toward me joyously ("Oh boy, he'll be glad to see us! He'll pet us and everything!"), jumping on me and crashing against my rod and the one tall boot I hadn't put on yet but had balanced before me in the muck. Then they went crashing and gallumphing in the water, romping in the muck along the shore and certainly scaring away any fish that might have been there.

I began making my way toward the water. I had expected there to be some muck, but I was sinking in over my knees at each step. It was horrendous. I persisted for fifteen minutes or so, hoping to find some firmer footing, but it got worse, not better.

As I turned away from the water, I noticed that I had attached the fly to the leader in such a way that I would have to take it off in order to put the two halves of the rod together.

And so on back home through the woods.

But then I went down to Drury Pond and went out alone in the old canoe. It was early evening. The pond was perfectly smooth and quiet. I paddled the length of it, watching a beaver swim across. I got quite close to him before he dived, with a resounding *thwack* of his tail. For the next hour, while I cast for pickerel, the beaver crossed and recrossed fairly nearby, occasionally becoming alarmed and diving, but then resuming his work/swim. A very handsome large loon, one we hear uphill at the house every day and every evening, swam placidly not far from me. Red winged blackbirds walked on the lily pads.

[NEIGHBORS]

THE CEMETERY—TWO YEARS LATER

The rhythm of work, talk—but everybody pitches *right* in. The place terribly overgrown in just two years—maple whips seem to grow four feet a year. People stop and talk when they want to. About ten people. Two power cutters. Butch Graves wanted to show off the capabilities of the Husqvarna bush cutter, which he sells. And it *is* good. Hartley with his smaller rig. Those two worked steadily and hard for three hours, one lunch break.

Dick's stories of mowers—forcing the guy in front to move faster for fear of getting his heels cut. Playing tricks like that.

"The good mowers, oh they mowed better than the machines. Not a blade sticking up, everything an even two inches.

"Young fellas today whack at it, but that's not the way—just a long, smooth, steady stroke, not too fast, not too slow."

Dick talked about sharpening the sickle bar of a mowing machine. At lunch break you sharpened it on a wheel with a wedge surface. Scythe blades were *long,* you put them on the stone walls to temper— they took a fantastic edge, "a skill you don't see today."

They wear clean work clothes (Ronnie's dark brown pants and shirt); I wear old clothes, rather dirty.

The bodies are oriented east-west, "so that when they sit up at the Judgment Day, they'll see their Maker face to face." They lie between a headstone and a footstone. The inscriptions are on the outer face of the headstone.

Dick, of the cemetery: "These were all fields, nice fields. Hamlin kept the cemetery mowed. I mowed it by scythe in 1934—that was the last time.

"There was a foundation made for the church of granite blocks, but they never did build on it. By then there was more and more going on down in the Intervale, so they had a big fight about it and built the church down there."

Jules Vernessoni comes up every year and puts flags on the three graves of Revolutionary War soldiers. I asked Hartley why Jules did this. "Well, he lives nearby. And I guess because he was a soldier himself."

During lunch break everyone rested by the stone wall, telling jokes, drinking beer and fruit juice. They kidded me as I took notes from some headstones. "Writin' your next book, Gawdge?" "Lookin' for a vacancy, Gawdge?" "You know what the undertaker says—get a lot while you can."

Hartley: "They say we're cuttin' a little faster than the forest grows now. A couple o' years ago we were behind by five percent, now we're supposed to be ahead—but when you see how this place grows up it's hard to believe."